Vadim E. Gippenreiter

TEXT BY
Robin Magowan

FABLED CITIES OF CENTRAL ASIA

Samarkand, Bukhara, Khiva

CASSELL

To Carol

EDITOR: **Jacqueline Decter**
DESIGNER: **Nai Chang**
PRODUCTION EDITOR: **Amy Handy**
PRODUCTION SUPERVISOR: **Hope Koturo**

Captions by Roya Marefat
Map by Sophie Kittredge

ACKNOWLEDGMENTS
You cannot travel in Soviet Central Asia without a certain amount of help. I was fortunate in finding, in Mikhail Anikst, Vladimir Pavlov, and Jean-Francois Valet, three urbane and witty friends who got me where I needed to go.
I was also fortunate in finding a caring editor in Jacqueline Decter.

FRONT COVER: Samarkand at night
BACK COVER: The Shir Dar madrasah, Samarkand
PAGES 2 AND 3: The Gur Emir mausoleum, Samarkand
PAGES 4 AND 5: Kalyan Square, Bukhara
PAGES 6 AND 7: Panorama of Khiva
FRONTISPIECE: Camels traversing a poppy field in the Badkhyz Reserve, Turkmenia.

The photographs on pages 61–72 are reproduced from Hugues Krafft, *A Travers le Turkestan Russe: Ouvrage illustré de deux cent soixante-cinq gravures* (Paris: Hachette, 1902). Courtesy of the General Research Division, The New York Public Library, Astor, Lenox and Tilden Foundations. The assistance of the library's Slavic and Baltic Division is gratefully acknowledged.

First published in the United Kingdom in 1990

Cassell Publishers Limited
Artillery House, Artillery Row
LONDON SW1P 1RT

Copyright © 1989 Abbeville Press, Inc.
Photographs copyright © 1989 Vadim Gippenreiter

Distributed in Australia by
Capricorn Link (Australia) Pty Limited,
PO Box 665, Lane Cove, NSW 2066

British Library Cataloguing in Publication data
Magowan, Robin
    Fabled cities of Central Asia : Samarkand, Bukhara, Khiva.
    1. Uzbekistan. Description & Travel
    I. Title II. Gippenreiter, Vadim
    915.8'704854

ISBN 0-304-31886-8

Typeset by David E. Seham Associates, Inc.
Printed and bound in Singapore

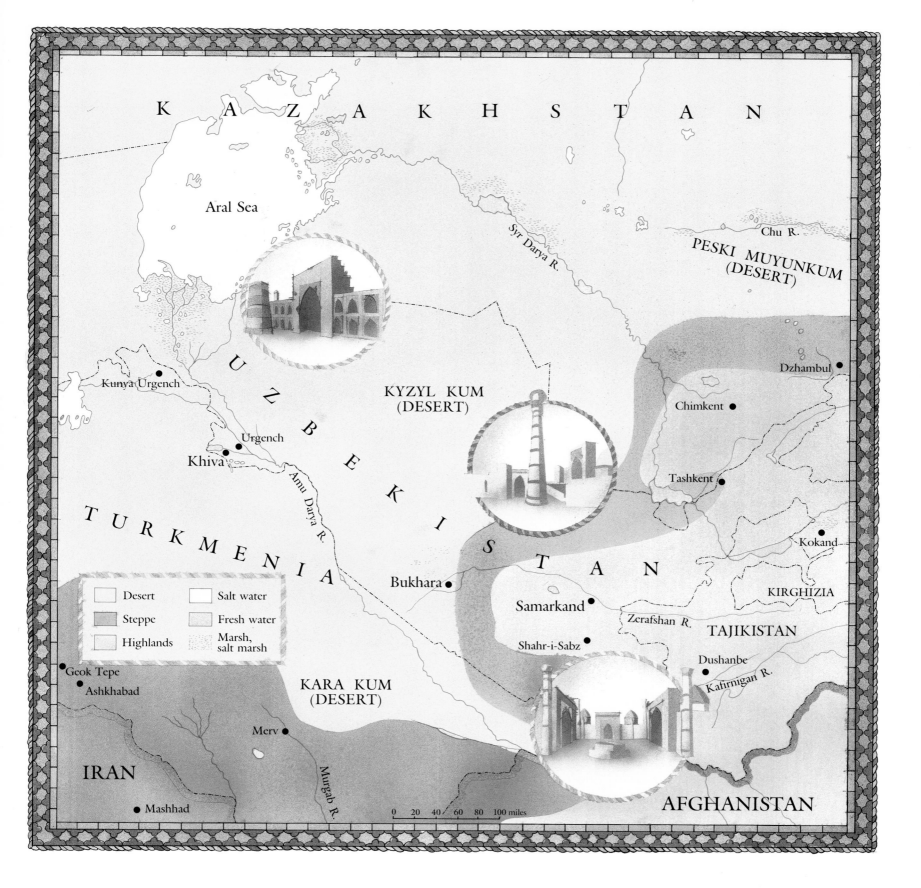

K A Z A K H S T A N

Aral Sea

Syr Darya R.

Chu R.

PESKI MUYUNKUM
(DESERT)

U Z B E K I S T A N

Kunya Urgench

KYZYL KUM
(DESERT)

Dzhambul

Chimkent

Urgench

Khiva

Amu Darya R.

Tashkent

Kokand

T U R K M E N I A

Bukhara

KIRGHIZIA

Samarkand

Zerafshan R.

TAJIKISTAN

Shahr-i-Sabz

Dushanbe

Kafirnigan R.

Desert	Salt water
Steppe	Fresh water
Highlands	Marsh, salt marsh

Geok Tepe

Ashkhabad

KARA KUM
(DESERT)

IRAN

Merv

Murgab R.

Mashhad

0 20 40 60 80 100 miles

AFGHANISTAN

C O N T

ENTS

❈ INTRODUCTION ❈

Not so long ago we could still judge a civilization by its cities. "Earth has not anything to show more fair," Wordsworth could murmur, looking out from a London bridge. Nowadays looking at the same view it's not his "cloud-capped towers" that we behold, but an updated version of Blake's "dark satanic mills," only now it's us, chained by our cars, who are being dragged round and round. There may still be a few for whom the object of travel consists of a great city's shops, galleries, restaurants, and theaters. But most of us, if we want to go somewhere to die, would rather choose Nepal or Bali than the Bay of Naples. The city is not the siren of old.

The notion of a planet on which our constructions are only a fraction of the general glory may be salutary in the long run. In the short, it works against the cities. If they are dying it is less, I suspect, because of the various blights we have unleashed than because we have lost Wordsworth's knack of seeing them as longed-for havens created from our dreaming selves, our eyes and skin and bones.

Now and then some gifted child, or an Italo Calvino, can put this aright, dreaming up his cities afresh, one labyrinth more bewitching, more frightening, than the last. The rest of us, less imaginatively confident, may be condemned to travel—the farther, perhaps, the better. Out there, "east of the sun and west of the moon," at the edge, say, of a huge desert, circumstances change. Under the impact it may suddenly flash on us that the Garden of Eden is simply another name for the first city. Oh, we say, seeing it with a desert traveler's eyes, so that's what a city is—*paradise*—the Old Persian for "walled garden." Extend the walls far enough and you have a city.

Eden has vanished in the sands, but we can still feel something of that resonance in the great desert paradises of Soviet Central Asia—Samarkand, Bukhara, and Khiva. Not only are they centers of an important civilization, one that may still have something to say to us, but they remain that increasingly rare thing, beautiful cities. If we want to rekindle our imaginations, it is hard to imagine a better trio with which to start.

To us in the West, cities are fixed, palpable things, built of rock, not fine-blown dust. Put one down and chances are that it will stay there. Bruges may become Bruges-la-Morte when the North Sea moves away, but it does not abandon its towers and canals to go chasing after the receding water. In Central Asia cities tend to lead a more spectral existence. Stuck out there at the Back of Beyond, in a space that could almost be imagined as sky itself, they come to occupy a fabled reality of their own.

To the desert traveler the city was nothing more or less than a name, an article of faith. And it was this name that you tied to the

The Ishratkhaneh, "House of Pleasure," in Samarkand was constructed in 1464. The burial site of Timurid princesses, it was endowed by the wife of the Timurid ruler Abu Said. Its remarkable *pishtaq*, a tripartite portal, led into a paved central hall that was capped by a double dome. The unusually high drummed outer dome collapsed in the earthquakes of 1897 and 1903.

The Silk Road that connected China to the West passed through the barren lands of Central Asia. Only the camel laden with valuable goods could withstand the harsh desert climate.

PAGE 17
The Shir Dar madrasah took its name from the lions (*shir* in Persian) on the spandrels of its *pishtaq* (portal). Built in 1619–35/36 by the Shaybanids, it is located in the Registan, Samarkand's central square, directly across from the famous Ulugh Beg madrasah. The Shir Dar is remarkable not for its plan, which is identical to that of the Ulugh Beg, but for its decoration. The images of the lion and the sun—depicted as a female face—represent the sun in the sign of Leo.

16

head of your mount, trusting that its magic syllables, sufficiently repeated, would by themselves guide you through the surrounding hell. For there was no way of knowing whether the city would still be there when and if you arrived. A Genghis Khan might have happened by. Or the river along which it nestled might have swept it away. Or it might simply have decided to up and move to a site, oh, two hundred kilometers away in the hope that conditions there would prove a little less chancy.

One would think such a Platonic abstraction might not have stood up to the grim reality: the five months on end of blistering heat; the constantly swirling dust; the horror of a proletariat in highly audible chains. But the traveler had put too much into his journey to be able to regard the city he reached as anything but paradise. And the local merchants, dependent on the flow of goods brought by the caravans, made sure that everything catered to the illusion. The sign PARADISE was there, written in welcoming green over the gardens, a belt of irrigated wealth that was the first visual sign of the city itself. Within the walled gates it appeared again, transfigured now into the dream-shapes of minarets, blue-glazed domes, and an imposing array of religious academies, madrasahs, where, likely as not, you would be put up, their arched entrances and perhaps the whole of their courtyard covered in an Elysian Field of endlessly shimmering tile.

Unable to credit your senses, you went from one miracle of blue to the next, eyeing in awe the courtiers in their robes of figured silk, perhaps now and then joining them in a bit of learned conversation. You might even have found yourself summoned to a private audience with the reigning prince, the two of you trading compliments that were nothing less than poems—a highly baited exchange in which one slip could mean your head.

By now it would have dawned on you that this so-called paradise was nothing more or less than an extraordinary stage set designed for one purpose and one purpose only—so that a prince could indulge himself in playing God. Hence the grandiose scale that the architecture projected, reminding you of your role: if not quite a speck of dust in the royal eye, then a chess pawn waiting to be moved, a puppet dangling on a string. Hence, too, the stylization of everything from speech to apparel, abetted in turn by an equally specialized backstage presence: craftsmen who did nothing but fashion water-silk swords, or the famous Bukhara Jewish silk dyers—the descendants of those borne off into captivity by Nebuchadnezzar—recognized by the purple dye on their hands.

As always the recourse to illusion had to be set off by moments of hyperrealism: a parade of moaning captives asked to pay with gouged

eyes for what a raiding party of their fellow tribesmen had recently inflicted on a passing caravan; or the screams of an adulterous woman being spun about in a burlap sack with a pair of wildcats. Such executions were invariably meted out in the square next to the royal palace. A charlatan might swallow a sword or walk on water. But an emir outshone them by taking away life itself. And here, as in all theater, everything lay in the manner.

From the great cities the vogue spread until there was hardly a petty despot who did not want to erect a theater of his own. And it stood to reason that nothing would satisfy him until he had triumphed on the boards of Samarkand itself. One has only to read Babur's memoirs to realize how central capturing Samarkand was to his self-image. Only at the end of his life, after thirty years of incessant efforts, did he allow himself to be consoled by the infinitely more tawdry prize of Northern India.

As a culture the Persian–Central Asian hardly compares with the Indo-Chinese, let alone our own Mediterranean. But if, like Jefferson and Stendhal, you regard the pursuit of happiness as being right up there with life and liberty as one of man's inalienable rights, or if you are intrigued by a culture that seeks to address not the human but the angel in ourselves, Central Asia may represent an avenue of hope. Why not live in a city set like a garden in the here and now?

This garden, like its Christian derivative, was not confined to any one particular *locus amoenus*. You could take it with you in the form of a carpet, or watch it glow over a whole city in the dome of a mosque. It might even blazon forth in the distichs of a calligraphed page. The idea behind it was basically Platonic. Only, in Central Asia, the world of essences that spilled and played in a sensational riot around you was the emanation not of some remote, cave-reflected "sun," but of your ruler, he whom you sat beside, whose smile lent your own its glow.

What saved the culture from elitist smugness was the sense of the ravaging desert that lay outside the walled enclosure. In this respect both the Hindu and the Persian are cultures of the moment. But whereas the Hindu moment extends all the way back to the beginnings of the globe, the Persian sees life as highly temporary and for that reason amoral. In Central Asia you might not become transparent, but you could become prismatic, and it was to that refinement of the sensibility that these connoisseurs of sensation strived.

In Central Asia we are not in the familiar world of history as simple Marxism conceives it, where progressive and counterprogressive forces push one another against the urban barricades. Here, at the desert edge of one or another violently carved-out empire, history rather resembles a cyclone. And there is no way of anticipating from what quarter it will blow in next. Here, at one moment, from the far reaches of the Black Sea, appear Alexander's Macedonian Greeks. They take to the theater as to the manor born, dressing in the best silks, staging drunken brawls in which the prince kills his best friend, and even marrying the local beauty, Roxana. A millennium later, out of the Arabian desert come the People of the Book. They last not much more than a century, but before they have gone, the fire and sword as faith have triumphed over the Zoroastrian-Nestorian legacy of good *and* evil, shadow *and* light. Another four centuries and it is the turn of the Scourges of God, as they call themselves, who have come on their little ponies down from the Gobi Desert. The Scourges disapprove of the theater. The sets are razed, and most of the backstage personnel find themselves liquidated. The next century and a half is not a good time for theater. But finally out of all the dust and ashes Central Asia generates a cyclone of its own in the person of Timur. In the course of thirty-five years he conquers everything from Damascus to Delhi, and an utterly rebuilt Samarkand becomes the center of what is now truly the world stage. It seems so hasty, one may feel, seeing one towering set after another collapse even before it is finished; but the whirlwind that Timur has set in motion is such that his sons and grandsons all the way to Babur in the sixth generation can go off looking for paradise-theaters of their own; ones with better building clay, a more earthquake-resistant soil. And they find them in Herat, in the Isfahan of Shah Abbas, all through Northern India. It is what historians are pleased to call the Timurid Renaissance.

For the cities along the Silk Road, Vasco da Gama's opening of the sea route to India and China was nothing short of catastrophic. How, after millennia of catering to the victims of necessity, were they to be satisfied with a public of the merely curious, an odd Russian Muraviev here, a Jenkinson there? At the same time the quality of those playing God began to get more and more petulant, more perverse. Troupes of painted dancing boys, a harem starting with girls of eight and nine—they were pensioned off once pregnant—were about all that an aspiring prince could delight and shock us with. Faced with cries for abolition, many reacted by declaring their cities off-limits. Any European venturing into Bukhara would be treated as a spy, clapped into the royal dungeons, and, if necessary, executed.

One would think that any number of players of the Great Game would have risen to the challenge. But the takers are surprisingly few. Two of them, Stoddart and Conolly, can't believe their eyes when, despite their ambassadorial papers and their officer status, they are arrested. At first, the emir is gentle with them, confining them to the

The Amu Darya River once flowed into the Caspian Sea through the area that is now the Kara Kum desert. The crescent-shaped dunes known as barchan are blown up to 60 feet high by the constant wind in the Repetek Preserve of Turkmenia.

house of his fat artillery commander. There, he knows, they will be well fed, and he may even hope that some of their military expertise will rub off on their host. But when his beautifully penned letter—a true poem from one epithet to the next—offering to conclude a treaty of alliance with the British brings no reply, other than an equivocal message from Lord Palmerston, the emir does what any exasperated poet in his place would do—he takes these two saints of the empire and confines them to his blackest hole. Perhaps he does not appreciate the difficulties of an understaffed bureaucracy in running an empire on which the sun never sets. Perhaps he believes in telepathy, in the sound of their screams getting through where all else has failed. In sheer desperation he starts fiddling with their religion: "If you will convert to Islam, I will . . ." not meaning a word of it, but trying to break down this stolid wall, these psychic inhibitions of theirs. Finally, realizing he himself is becoming too obsessed with this one poem, in utter despair he has them executed.

Even so, the arresting of the two officers is so unbelievable that a man of the cloth, Joseph Wolff, takes it upon himself to journey all the way to Bukhara in an effort to ascertain what has actually befallen them. When the emir claps him in prison, too, he saves himself only with another act of theater—by playing mad.

Forewarned is forearmed, and in 1863 the Hungarian Arminius Vambéry limps in, disguised as a begging dervish from Constantinople. He is a gifted linguist, able to speak not only the languages of Europe but Persian, Turkish, and Arabic with perfect native fluency. His gripping account of his terrifying journey from the Caspian Sea across the Kara Kum desert to Khiva, then onward across the Kyzyl Kum to Bukhara and Samarkand, is indispensable for anyone interested either in the Turkmen nomads or the extraordinary theater of these city-states.

Reading Vambéry, it is hard to realize that there is a Russian expeditionary force drawing near, determined to close down this blood-curdling anachronism once and for all. In 1868 Bukhara falls. Five years later it is Khiva's turn. Is the slave mart pulled down, turned into its present-day bazaar? No, the clanking of chains goes on, and the attempted flights into the desert, until 1917.

One of the first things the Russians notice upon capturing Khiva is the fine Egyptian-type cotton that has flourished for several millennia. Imagine, they think, the yields that could be obtained with the coarser American variety. This succeeds so well that in no time Khwarezm is outproducing every province in Russia, a situation that holds to the present day. The problem is, of course, that you need a considerable labor force to pick cotton, one available only in the form of slaves. This puts the Russians in a bit of a quandary since Alexander II eman-

A TURKMAN

A TURKMAN

AN UZBEK

A TURKMAN

A TAJIK WOMAN

A TURKMAN WOMAN

A TURKMAN WOMAN

Centuries of migration and invasion have populated Central Asia with people of many races, including the Mongol-featured Uzbeks, the Indo-Iranian Tajiks, and the Turkic Turkmen. Although their languages are very different, they have co-existed for such a long time that most speak more than one language.

PAGES 24–25
The steppes of Central Asia provide the nomadic tribes with vast pastures for their herds of karakul sheep. These sheep, with their characteristic long and curly fleece, graze on the scant vegetation and are the nomads' source of food, milk, and clothing. Turkmen wear protective caps made from the coarsest part of the fleece.

23

cipated the serfs in 1862. Forced to choose between their civilizing mission and their need for cotton, the Russians decide that the conquest hasn't happened. Back onto his golden throne as absolute master goes the khan, back into their shackles go the cotton pickers, and theatrical life goes on the same as ever until the Bolsheviks finally arrive to set matters right.

In the following years of civil war Samarkand finds itself siding with the Reds—anything to get free of Bukhara!—and the victors reward the city by making Samarkand the seat of the new dispensation. A ring of universities, medical schools, hospitals comes to encircle the city. Water is brought in from the mountains to irrigate the cotton fields in such quantity that the climate is drastically changed. Skies that rarely saw a cloud are now semipermanently overcast, and the famous golden light made possible by the city's two-thousand-mile distance from the nearest sea also becomes a thing of the past. Despite limiting Samarkand to a single enormous cotton factory, the pollution is such that the mountains near Timur's birthplace of Shahr-i-Sabz, the Green City, have become well nigh invisible.

While Samarkand prospered, Bukhara and Khiva were left undeveloped in the hope that they would wither and die. In the case of Bukhara, one of the holiest cities in Islam, one can understand the Soviets' reluctance. They did not want to touch off another powder keg. They succeeded so well that when Ella Maillart visited Bukhara in 1932, a city of 200,000 had dwindled to a mere 40,000.

By the end of World War II this policy had come to seem a bit like killing off the goose that lays the golden egg. Even today Moscow has reason to look like what it is, an impoverished, badly kept up Third World city. The pre-1917 Russian class structure of czar, boyars, bureaucrats, and serfs was not one geared toward individual commercial enterprise. But Bukhara, out at the edge of the desert, is a city that has always had to live by its commercial and theatrical wits. There was a craft tradition ready to be adapted to the needs of Soviet industry. Nor was it long before a new, not inelegant city had sprung up outside the old walls.

About ten years ago, as a result of falling oil prices, the Soviet Union was obliged to start developing new sources of hard currency. It was inevitable that it should recognize the tourist value inherent in these three magical names. No matter that a number of the great sets had crumbled. They would be restored, and what couldn't would be re-created from scratch. One may often feel that this "museum in the open," as one Soviet coffee-table book calls it, is but another name for a ghost town, or the tourist ghetto that it is slated to become. But while waiting for a true openness to develop—and nothing less than full autonomy will do—we can be grateful for a glimpse at three of the world's great names.

Moscow

Getting to see the great garden cities of Central Asia has never been easy. Even in recent years the only way for a Westerner to visit them has been as a package tourist. For many, being shepherded around in a group from one monument to the next may not be all that bad. At least you are there, where so few Western eyes have ever been, and you are not being bankrupted in the process.

For the traveler who wants to linger a bit and see something of the city life, the culture that gave rise to these outbursts of monumental building, getting there is apt to be a good deal more complicated. For one, the Intourist system is not geared to the needs of the private traveler. You have to make do with whatever space is left over. And once there you may still find your ability to move about rather restricted. You have to spend the night, for instance, in your Intourist hotel. And if you strike off on your own to visit an outlying off-limits shrine, or a town not on your itinerary, you may find yourself on the next plane back to Moscow.

I had applied for a month's visa, listing Samarkand, Bukhara, and Khiva as the three cities I wanted to visit. I had neglected to discuss any of this with Intourist in advance, assuming that my hosts at the Moscow end were taking care of my travel arrangements. The two shepherds from the sponsoring agency who met me at the airport—a new arrival is not encouraged to wander about Moscow on his own—told me that I was in real danger of being put on the next flight back to London. Only at the last minute was this threat averted and a hotel room found, a fifteen-minute bus ride across the river from the Kremlin. There I would have to stay until my travel arrangements were complete.

As it turned out, this would take another eight days. But the time was far from wasted. I had traveled in Bulgaria and Hungary twenty years before, and more recently in the north of China, experiences I had never succeeded in getting down on paper, perhaps because I found myself too detached from the real life there. This time I was determined to refuse the invitations of the passing taxis, the glamour of the subways, and do what I could to walk. You find that it can be done, of course, but it leaves you, leaves everyone, exhausted. Those haggard faces, empty suitcase in hand, eyes riveted to the ground, tell you how hard life is here in the embattled north. Above all they testify to what

Tajik women often wear long tunics over baggy pants *(sharovary)*.

the mammoth scale of the city, with its endless blocks, its pitted concrete sidewalks, and the lack of anywhere to stop, has been doing to them.

Vadim Gippenreiter

While waiting for my travel arrangements to be completed I called on the photographer Vadim Gippenreiter in the hope that I could persuade him to accompany me to Central Asia. Since I was seeing it through the eye of his camera it would help to have him there, steering me to what I needed to explain.

The Ansel Adams of the Soviet Union was there to greet me at the door of the Sparrow Hills apartment that he shares with his painter son, his pale blue eyes popping mischievously out of a wiry-haired, lean, virtually ageless face. He was dressed in the tracksuit that has become part of his legend (he jogs five miles a day, and no one I know has ever seen him in anything else). We were up very high in the Moscow air, on the sixteenth floor of a seventeen-floor apartment building. The walls that weren't glass reverberated with paintings—jagged, highly textured, early Jackson Pollock–like swirls—not his son's work, he explained, but a friend's who now resides in Italy. The record shelves held an extensive jazz collection. On the table was a sumptuously laid out tea: cheese, walnuts, cake, and a local version of éclair. Though Vadim has done books on seemingly every part of the Soviet Union, he has never traveled abroad and doesn't speak any Western European language.

As for accompanying me to Central Asia, that was, he explained, out of the question. He had a project on the recently restored Russian churches of the north to complete before the June millennial celebrations. Besides, it was the wrong time of year. Not only was the light better in late summer, a blue of sky making you understand what a glazed dome might be about, but it was then, when the bazaar was most teeming with color, that the majority of the folk spectacles took place: weddings virtually every day, falconry out in the desert, and the notorious *buzkashi*, a lethal game played with a sheep's head—two 150-man sides mounted on horseback.

"Isn't it hot then?" I asked, put off by the prospect of an air so much hotter than the blood.

"It's a dry heat," he explained, "and everything is shaded so you are never in it directly."

When I asked how he had happened to go to Central Asia, he explained that during the war the Moscow Art Institute was evacuated to Samarkand. He had been an athlete before the war, Soviet downhill skiing champion in 1940, and was then studying sculpture. "But all of us sculpture students were obliged to do what we called 'holy figures.' You can imagine how well I did at it," he added with a chuckle.

Architecture, of course, is not that far removed from sculpture, especially Central Asian architecture with all its different planes, volumes, fake ceilings, and real ceilings. In the process of studying it Vadim found himself picking up a camera. "I spent almost two months alone photographing the Shah-e-Zindeh mausoleum complex," he said. "You know, the people there don't like Russians. But seeing me clambering about the roofs all that time, they got used to me."

It is hard to say how much Vadim's athletic discipline, that training toward a specific event, has influenced his photography. But he differs from most photographers in knowing exactly the effect he wants. The rest, as he says, is patience, how much time on your hands and knees or wriggling about on your back you are willing to put into it. What emerges, however, is an extraordinary poetry, as if the great buildings themselves were speaking to us directly from centuries away. And for all their bulk, their centuries of notoriety, it is a very private, mysteriously shadowed dialogue they conduct, one all the more persuasive in the absence of any human mediation, the people occurring only when needed to suggest scale.

Over the years Vadim has developed a great respect for the Persian-speaking Tajik people who dominate the commercial life of Samarkand and Bukhara. And he lays it squarely at the feet of their women. Even when they look the same, he says, you can always tell a Tajik by her carriage. Uzbek women walk behind their men, eyes on the ground. The Tajik woman walks often enough ahead, staring straight at you. "I almost married one," he tells me. "University background, very well connected, and I'd be a rich man today if I had. But she didn't want to move to Moscow and I didn't want to spend the rest of my life in Central Asia."

Qutham ibn-Abbas, the cousin of the Prophet Mohammed, is said to be buried in the Shah-e-Zindeh necropolis in Samarkand. His shrine is one of the holiest places in Central Asia and the faithful make regular pilgrimages to it.

❊ SAMARKAND ❊

Of the great theater cities, Samarkand, two time zones to the east of Moscow, makes as good a place to touch down as any. The golden light that traveler after traveler once remarked on may be a thing of the past, but the city could not be more pleasant. Its geographical situation at the hub of a natural mountain-ringed crossroads, together with its vast oasis, watered by the two great rivers of Central Asia, the Amu Darya (the Oxus of classical antiquity, for the Arabs one of the four rivers of paradise) and the Zerafshan or Strewer of Gold, have much to do with it. As does its height: 2,200 feet may not be all that high, but it is 1,600 feet higher than Bukhara two hundred miles to the west, and the difference shows. And, like Rome, the city it most resembles, it has the advantages that come from being scattered about on a series of hills. Wherever you look there is a minaret or a glazed dome popping out, its blue more than rivaling the sky. However hot it is—and temperatures can rise as high as 45 to 47 degrees centigrade (120 Fahrenheit)—there is usually a semblance of wind, and you have only to step into the shade to feel a cooling dryness. Here, so far from the sea, the motes of swirling dust create a translucency in which you can not only see unusually far, but the objects themselves—a beard, a shawl, the entrance arch of a mosque—take on a soft, sculpted patina. At dawn, at dusk, there is nothing quite like it.

This dust being blown off the mountains in the form of loess gives the oasis its fertility. Virtually anything will grow in it. That for the past hundred years the main crop has been cotton, rather than melons or any one of a number of grapes, seems something of a pity when the Soviet Union is having such difficulty feeding itself. But cotton means big rubles, and it is hard to begrudge the peasants their prosperity.

If the fertility of the surrounding oasis is the prime source of Samarkand's continuing prosperity, it was its position at the forking of the Silk Road from China (one strand proceeding south to Afghan Bactria and thence to India, the other southwest to Herat and the Caspian) that made it from time immemorial the Rome of Central Asia. When Alexander arrived in 329 B.C. it was already a considerable city with an impregnable citadel and an outer rampart measuring fourteen kilometers in circumference.

The region, known to Kipling as the Back of Beyond, has gone in time by many names. To the people of the classical world it was Transoxiana; to the Arabs it was the Land between the Rivers; to the Elizabethans, Tartary. For his part the celebrated fourteenth-century Moroccan traveler Ibn Batuta referred to it as Turkestan, a name it would keep until 1930 when Stalin renamed it Uzbekistan in honor of the Turkish-speaking, Mongol-featured Uzbek tribe that, from the mid-sixteenth century on, has dominated the countryside.

This dramatic panorama of the city looks toward the Registan and the Bibi Khanum mosque. In the foreground is a mausoleum known as Ruhabad, built in 1380 by Timur for the saint Burhanud-Din Sagardgi. In its simplicity and modest size it comes closer to the Shah-e-Zindeh mausoleums than to the majestic and gigantic monuments of Timur's later reign.

 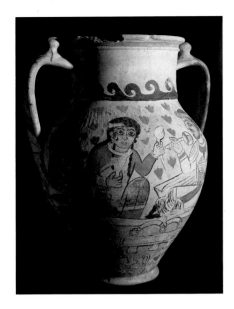 

In 329–327 B.C. Alexander conquered Central Asia. Artifacts found by archaeologists testify to the influence of Hellenism on Central Asian art. Left: The polychromed clay head from Khalchayan can be dated to the first century B.C. It resembles classical Greek representations of Hercules. Right: The second-century A.D. carving on a stele shares features of frontality and drapery treatment with Palmyrene reliefs. Center: The fifth-century vase from Merv, another ancient artistic center of Central Asia, depicts images of courtly life and shows influences of Sassanian art.

The original inhabitants were Sogdians, an Indo-European-speaking people. Despite a number of razings and the incursions by a seemingly endless swarm of Turkish-speaking nomads, they still make up a considerable proportion of the population of both Samarkand and Bukhara, large enough for there to be the beginnings of a movement (akin to that among the Armenians of Nagorno-Karabakh) to include the two cities in an expanded Tajikistan.

In appearance these Tajiks are close to the Afghans of Herat; they lack the blue-black hair, enormous noses, and arching eyebrows of the typical Iranian and are generally taller. As to how they have managed to retain their cultural identity, you have only to come out of the bazaar and try to saunter down an old street lined with mulberry trees and two-story nineteenth-century houses to be confronted by a man telling you that you have wandered into a cul-de-sac. When it keeps happening every few feet you begin to realize what their notions of privacy may be about.

The Zoroastrian city that bewitched Alexander was known as Maracanda. When we next hear of it, after its conquest by the armies of the Arab caliphate under Qutham ibn-Abbas, it is called Afrasiab. In 1220 Genghis Khan turns the hill of Afrasiab into its present cemetery. What happens next is open to conjecture. Legends abound about all sorts of Samars and Shamars—destroyers of cities, finders of water. I would like to believe that Sa, possibly from Sart, the name the town dwellers called themselves until 1917 (and which, despite its pejorative connotations—it now refers only to the merchant class—I have chosen to retain), was placed before Maracanda, a couple of *a*'s were dropped, and Samarkand was born.

Timur

Samarkand, the most silken of names, was almost enough. All that remained was for somebody to come along and rebuild it as the Rome of Central Asia. That person was Timur (1336?–1405), otherwise known as Tamerlane, the greatest conqueror the world has ever known.

As a historical figure Timur belongs to that not so rare type, the self-made athlete-businessman who has risen through the ranks. Only for Timur, sport was the deadly game of war. We are told that continual war of the sort Timur waged inevitably ends by bankrupting a nation and draining it of its life's blood. Under Timur, however, war unquestionably paid. His campaigns were organized as systematic lootings, with one set of acquisitions paving the way for the next.

We are used to regarding our warriors as people who are fighting for something—God, the rights of man, a war to end all wars, peace and prosperity, the American way of life. To Timur all that would have been arrant sentimentality. He fought for the sole purpose of staying in the field. And he brought to the art of war as single-minded a concentration as the world has ever seen. We may blanch at a ruthlessness that could order the slaughter of the whole male population of any city that dared to resist him. But that was the name of the game—kill or be killed—and after thirty-five years one would think the other side would have gotten some idea as to how the shots were being called. A man who had never once lifted a siege was not likely to grow impatient after a month and hasten off after easier prey. With his reputation on the line he did no more or less than what the circumstances required. And the same governing rationality held elsewhere, in the ex-rulers he kept on, in the lenient taxes he imposed. He was never vain or, like so many Central Asian despots, wantonly cruel.

It is hard not to admire a chieftain who, before proceeding into battle, would listen to the recital of a defeat suffered by one of his forebears as a result of self-satisfaction and insufficient preparation. A Sunni in the best sense, Timur made sure that the head always ruled alongside the heart. In his subjects the one failing he refused to countenance was dishonesty.

A Turkish speaker of part-Mongol extraction, Timur did not hail from Samarkand, but the pretty town of Shahr-i-Sabz several mountain passes away. But as a young warrior he seems to have conceived a passion for the Big City of a sort that one of us might entertain for the local ball team. When he conquered it, it was doing all right—up there in third or fourth place behind Urgench and Bukhara in the Central Asian League. Most rulers would have been satisfied with that; you

En route to Samarkand in 1404, Clavijo visited Shahr-i-Sabz, and was able to see Timur's sumptuous and ostentatious Aq Sarai palace, or White Palace. This majestic structure, grandiose in scale and elaborate in surface decoration, is typical of the buildings Timur commissioned. Craftsmen were purportedly brought from Khwarezm to work on it. Two great pylons and part of the walls are all that remain of the palace.

Although Shahr-i-Sabz never gained the political importance of Samarkand, Timur lavished great wealth upon his birthplace. The Dar us-Siadat was the mausoleum he built for both his spiritual teacher and his father; he also buried his own sons Jahangir and Omar Shaykh here. Plots of land nearby were allocated to noblemen who wanted to be in close proximity to this venerated mausoleum. The Dar us-Siadat was considered the mausoleum of Timurid princes before the Gur Emir in Samarkand replaced it. In the nineteenth century a mosque was added to this structure; it is still functioning.

can't buck tradition. But the fan in Timur wanted to take Samarkand to the top not only of the Central Asian League but of the All-Asian League as well. The object of his campaigns was, to be sure, new taxable domains and all the booty he and his men could stagger away with. But no matter how far afield he was he never stopped thinking about, and recruiting for, Team Samarkand: masons, tile layers, architects, now and then the odd intellectual or musician for his court. You can't help but feel that advancing Samarkand to its rightful spot as the number-one garden city preceded any notion of staking out a place for himself in the World Conquerors Record Book. It was only late in his career, when Samarkand's first-place position was assured—only China remained to be conquered—that he began to think of the benefits of a world under his sole leadership. "As there is one Allah in heaven," he argued, not implausibly, "so should there be but a single viceroy on earth."

There is a well-known story about Timur's summoning the great Persian poet Hafez in Shiraz. The poet, by then an old man, appeared before him dressed in tatters. Timur reminded him of his famous poem in which he says that he would give all of Bukhara's "vaunted gold, all the gems of Samarkand," for the sight of his beloved. "How dare you," Timur asked, "give away what is not yours, but mine?" Without missing a beat Hafez replied, pointing to his rags, "You see where such prodigality has gotten me."

Timur's own prodigality involved buildings. For another ruler, Samarkand's position on the Silk Road would have been enough; all he had to do was sit back and wait for the caravans to appear. But Timur knew that the merchants were also human beings, traveling the Golden Road for their pleasure and edification. To obtain their goods in the volume he craved he had to entice them—and in what better way than a show of domes? The buildings were in this sense the fifteenth-century equivalent of a Disney World. As one marvel succeeded another, one can imagine the curiosity mounting—what would Timur amaze us with next?

When the Spanish envoy Clavijo visited Samarkand in 1404, Timur's building was more or less complete. A deep moat encircled the whole city, which was guarded in turn by a many-towered, crenellated wall with ramparts wide enough in places for a rider to gallop along. From the great central hub of the Registan, broad thoroughfares radiated out to six gates. Beyond the walls lay thirteen parks full of summer palaces, fountains, and plunging terraces. In an astonishing twenty days Clavijo himself witnessed the demolition and construction of a huge bazaar running from the foot of the Bibi Khanum mosque down to the Amu Darya. Its central axis was lined with fountains and sur-

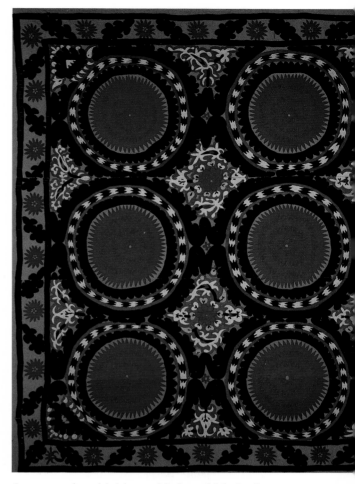

Suzan-work, a highly sophisticated kind of embroidery, is found throughout Central Asia. Symmetrical arrangements of colorful motifs, natural or geometrical, are hand-embroidered on cotton and silk.

The Shah-e-Zindeh (Living King) mauso-leum complex, looking east. The Timurid ar-istocracy wished to be buried in close proxim-ity to the shrine of the "Living King," Qutham ibn-Abbas, cousin of the Prophet Mohammed. The earliest construction on this site dates to the eleventh century. The mauso-leums themselves date from 1360 to 1434 and flank a narrow, sunken alley measuring about 265 feet in length, giving the site an urban feeling.

mounted by a series of cupolas that protected shoppers from the sun. In Samarkand itself, each trade had its own bazaar, and according to Babur, the city was unrivaled for the quality of its papermaking and its crimson damask.

Given the highly seismic terrain and the fact that the buildings were never anything but dust faced with mud, it is remarkable that anything should be left upright. Whatever loess does for agriculture, it does not make for very permanent building. Nonetheless a trio of outstanding structures has survived: the Shah-e-Zindeh necropolis complex, the enormous Bibi Khanum mosque, and the Gur Emir mausoleum in which Timur lies buried. Together they provide a fas-cinating testament to Timur himself and to the theater to which he aspired.

The Shah-e-Zindeh

Of the three remaining edifices, the Shah-e-Zindeh or "Living King," built between 1360 and 1434 on the site of an earlier complex on the southern slope of the ruined city of Afrasiab, is aesthetically the most rewarding. It commemorates the spot where Qutham ibn-Abbas, a cousin of the Prophet Mohammed and the founder of Islam in Central Asia, finding himself hemmed in on all sides by pursuers, discovered the earth opening under him in the form of a well—the well, obviously, of the living faith from which Central Asians are still drinking to this day. One can see it suiting the magus in Timur to have Qutham's well spout forth in such a wealth of blue from every angle of its hill.

37

To the west of the steep thirty-six-step stairway of the Shah-e-Zindeh is a group of structures known as Qazizadeh Rumi, or the double-cupola mausoleum. At the top of the stairway is the second *chahartaq* (four-pillar arch), which leads to the middle group of mausoleums.

The complex reveals Timur at his most politically astute. Needing to placate those who may have felt, as the imam of the Ismail al-Bokhari shrine said to me in regard to Khomeini, that "all this incessant warfare isn't very Muslim," he built a shrine honoring the local saint. But he chose to line the pathway leading up to it with a series of personal mausoleums—a sister here, a wife there. It thus became a bridge linking the founder of one order of enterprise with that of another.

From afar the Shah-e-Zindeh's domes invite you, their robin's-

The double-cupola mausoleum (first quarter of the fifteenth century) consists of a large square chamber attached to a smaller one. It holds a single cenotaph. Each chamber has a dome with a high drum upon which stylized Kufic inscriptions are applied in *banai* technique (geometric or calligraphic patterning formed by the arrangement of glazed and bisque tiles). For a long time this structure was believed to be the mausoleum of Timur's wet nurse and her daughter. Later it was mistakenly identified as the mausoleum of Ulugh Beg's famous astronomer, Qazizadeh Rumi, until Soviet archeologists excavated skeletons of women from the crypt.

egg blue standing out against the yellow browns of the surrounding city. Passing through the archway of a mosque you enter the mausoleum complex by way of an unusually wide, thirty-six-step stairway. Once at the top, and the elevation is as much spiritual as physical, you find yourself in what amounts to a little village. Here, on each side of the sunken walkway leading to Qutham's tomb, lie the dead whom Timur and his family have chosen to honor. Each has his shrine, his set of rooms as it were, but the interiors, for all their highly ribbed, five-pointed-star domes and dripping "stalactite" corner vaulting, take

PAGE 40
The ceiling of the smaller chamber of the double-cupola mausoleum is decorated in an elaborate *muqarnas* (stalactite) design. A remarkable example of Timurid workmanship, the *muqarnas* ceiling shows the masterful use of geometry that was unique to Islamic architecture. Conceptually the dome was the symbol of the cosmic universe—the dome of heaven. The dynamic play of light and shade in the cells of these stalactite shapes is reinforced by the light penetrating through the four windows at different times of day. In contrast to the lush blue of the outer dome, with its ornate and decorative designs, the walls of the stalactite design are painted white.

This detail of the base of a column in the Shah-e-Zindeh is an example of engraved and relief-glazed terra cotta, sometimes called ganch. The geometric and floral designs are typical of Islamic architectural ornament.

second place to the outer façade's fanfare of color. By now you have forgotten about the domes, which have disappeared from sight; you are enclosed in and carried along by this new order of tile. Alternating vertical strips of blue, then blue and white—rather like the borders of a carpet—work in contrast to a ganch, or silhouette-carved high relief, in which turquoise-threaded flowers jut from a lapis lazuli background. Above you, from another archway of the same façade, tile flowers peer out, birdlike.

As you walk along you can't help but note the advancing tile technique: a mere twelve years later the flanking panels have become much wider, allowing a new, much more resonant blue to sing against the explosions of orange and green and an equally new background black. Tribal restraint has given way to what might seem outright joy,

Climbing up the steep steps, one comes upon the second *chahartaq* (eighteenth–nineteenth centuries). Four-pillar vaulting of this kind dates back to the pre-Islam fire temples of Zoroastrianism. Here the *chahartaq* serves as a transition or gateway to the middle group of buildings in the ensemble.

The entrance of the Shadi Mulk Agha mausoleum (foreground) is directly across from the Shirin Bek Agha mausoleum. The Shadi Mulk was constructed in 1372 by order of Timur's older sister, Turkan Qutlugh Agha. The names of its architects and craftsmen are inscribed on the entry portal as a testimony to their status. The mausoleum's richly carved tile work and glazed-brick ornamentation are unique. The mausoleum of Shirin Bek Agha, Timur's other sister, was built in 1385–86. It is unusual for its extensive use of mosaic faience and its inscriptions—quotations from Socrates.

The range and variety of the Shah-e-Zindeh's domes are partially visible in this view, looking east. On the left and right are the fluted domes of the Emirzadeh and Shadi Mulk mausoleums. Their original tile decoration has been lost. In the background is the round dome of Shirin Bek with its distinctive diaper-pattern design.

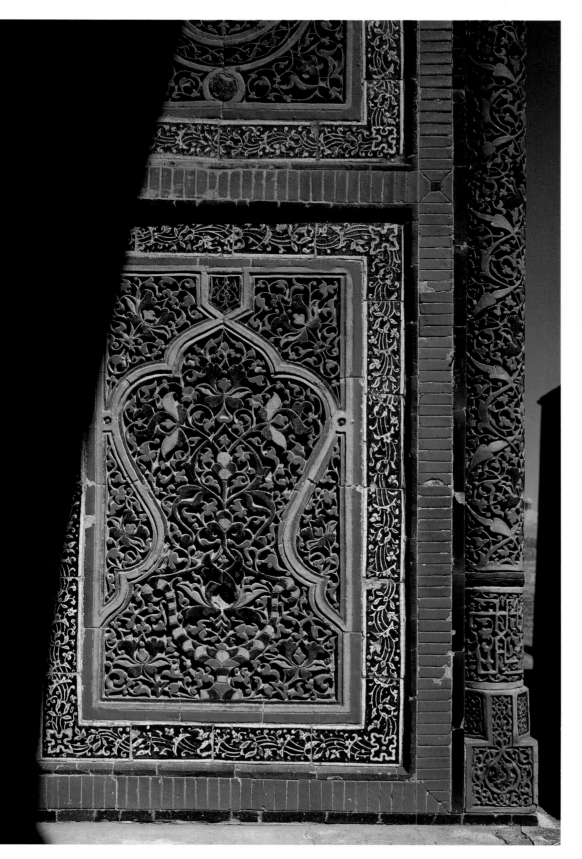

Detail of the inscriptions on the façade of the Emirzadeh (1386). Located on the western side of the alley immediately beyond the second *chahartaq*, this mausoleum contains nine cenotaphs. The names of the buried, however, remain a mystery. The exterior wall revetment combines carved glazed terra cotta and underglaze painted tiles.

A trilobe medallion forms the repeated motif in the decoration of the inner portal of the Shadi Mulk mausoleum. Its intricate carving and vegetal ornamentation, reminiscent of a Persian garden, brings to mind the symbolism of the tomb as garden. In Arabic literature the tomb is in fact often referred to as *Rawdat* (garden).

45

Looking south along the sunken alley, in the foreground is an octagonal structure believed to date back to the 1430s. A number of graves were uncovered in the underlying crypt by Soviet archeologists. The plan of this structure is quite unusual for the buildings on the site, most of which have square plans. An open octagonal pavilion, the building is not attached to the structures flanking it. Buff-tone brick forms an alternating pattern with colored glazed brick. The structure was no doubt capped by a dome that has collapsed; only the inner dome remains. The dome of the Shirin Bek mausoleum rises behind it and in the distance are the domes of the double-cupola mausoleum.

The buildings on the west side of the alley, looking north. In the foreground is the edifice referred to as the Mausoleum of Ustad Nasefi. Next to it is the Unknown mausoleum no. 2, which is adjacent to the Emir Burundaq mausoleum. In the background is the dome of the Tuman Agha mausoleum.

Detail of Ustad Nasefi (c. 1370). This mausoleum was named after its master builder. Although the name of its patron is missing, the exterior decoration is the manifestation of the patron's piety. Ornamental bands of star-shaped and cross-shaped motifs are filled with stylized Kufic inscriptions from the Koran. In places the underglaze painted tile decoration is still visible. The interior of the structure is also ornately decorated with tile. In the distance, the reconstruction of the Bibi Khanum mosque can be seen.

Detail of the *pishtaq* of the Unknown mausoleum, or Mausoleum of 1361. A deeply recessed, repetitive motif, executed in a calligraphic manner, forms a decorative band on either side of the *pishtaq*.

The blue-tiled dome of the Tuman Agha mausoleum, seen from the roof of the shrine of Qutham ibn-Abbas. This photograph reveals the diversity of vaulting techniques used in the Shah-e-Zindeh necropolis.

The Tuman Agha mausoleum (1405–6). Tuman Agha, one of Timur's favorite wives, was the daughter of his general Amir Musa. She was the patron not only of the mausoleum but also of the adjacent mosque and small service room. The mausoleum itself shares many characteristics with the Shirin Bek mausoleum, including the generous use of mosaic faience. The name of the calligrapher who adorned the structure, Shaykh Mohammed b. Hajji Bandgir al-Tughrai Tabrizi, is inscribed.

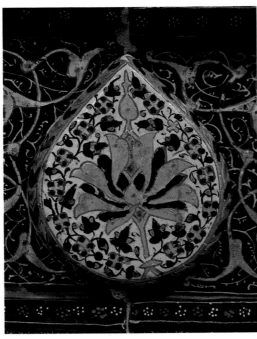

PAGE 52
Top left: Cenotaph of Qutham ibn-Abbas. The raison d'être of the Shah-e-Zindeh ensemble is the shrine of Qutham ibn-Abbas, cousin of the prophet Mohammed, who brought Islam to Central Asia. Legend has it that Qutham is alive and living in a well. Timur rebuilt part of the shrine as well as the accompanying mosque, mausoleum, minaret, and numerous chambers. The multitiered cenotaph of Qutham, who died in 676–77, is ornately decorated in the *lajavardina* technique (a cobalt-blue base with gilded underglaze painting in geometric and floral designs). Koranic phrases and reverent sayings about the "Living King" are inscribed in lavish calligraphy.

Bottom left: Detail of the tear-shaped medallions on the cenotaph of Qutham ibn-Abbas. The cenotaph was probably made in 1335 during the redecoration of the shrine.

Right: Entrance to the shrine of Qutham ibn-Abbas. The intricately carved elmwood doors exemplify the technical virtuosity of the craftsmen Timur imported to Samarkand. Seyyid Yusuf Shirazi carved his name and date of execution, 1405, on the mullion of the door. The upper insets are elaborately inscribed in *thulth* script.

color for color's sake. Even the gold inscriptions have become a dance in themselves, of cursive letters among flowers. And new colors keep being added. Here, for instance, is a façade featuring tiny red-centered flowers and lots of green. Yet it's the yellow that, for good or bad, stands out, catches the eye by its novelty.

Compared to Timur's later work, there is nothing in the least pretentious about the Shah-e-Zindeh complex. Yet in the joy of its carving, in the blue-purple vibrations that bounce against your eyes, it is like coming upon, as Joseph Brodsky notes, an outcropping of ''corals in the desert.'' Such is the feeling of intimacy and serenity produced by this masterpiece of scale and color that it's hard not to believe that you have stepped into the soul of Timur's empire.

PAGE 53
Located in the north courtyard of the Shah-e-Zindeh are the Tuman Agha mausoleum (left), the Unknown mausoleum or Mausoleum of 1361 (right), and the Khwaja Ahmed mausoleum, built in the 1360s (center). Only the façade of the Khwaja Ahmed mausoleum remains. Both the Mausoleum of 1361 and the Khwaja Ahmed are exemplary of the type of ornamentation that was prevalent in the mid-fourteenth century—carved glazed terra cotta and glazed brick.

Not long after its completion in 1404, the dome of the Bibi Khanum mosque collapsed. A contemporary chronicler wrote: "Its dome would have been unique had it not been for the heavens, and unique would have been its portal had it not been for the Milky Way." Here the dome is seen before restoration.

54

The Bibi Khanum Mosque

In contrast, the Bibi Khanum mosque (1399–1404) finds Timur at his most Cecil B. De Mille. From his successful Indian campaign he brings back ninety-seven teams of elephants. What besides war will they be used for? Immediately the notion of a mosque, grander, more opulent than anything in all of Asia, springs to his mind. Dedicating it to his senior consort, Saray Mulk Khanum, he has it built next to the bazaar, emphasizing a fertile connection that has always accompanied the spread of Islam.

There are descriptions of the old man himself personally overseeing the construction and, from his place on the scaffold, tossing down coins and scraps of meat to the workers below. As can be imagined, the work progresses at breakneck speed. In the marble quarries forty kilometers away, stone pillars are cut, 480 in all, and transported to Samarkand by the elephants. In three months the minarets are already erected. At one point Timur decides that the adjoining bazaar is too cramped and orders a new one to be built (the broad, fountain-lined thoroughfare described by Clavijo) in twenty days. On his return from another campaign, he finds the central portal not imposing enough and has it demolished and a new one built in its place.

The vault of the central dome may not have rivaled heaven itself, as one court poet put it, and the central portal may not have outshone the Milky Way, but the Bibi Khanum was big. (The modern replica is about a third smaller.) Babur reports that one gold inscription could be read a mile away. The three inner rooms were so large that to keep the walls from buckling the intervening niches had to be filled in and replaced with buttresses. Even before the mosque was consecrated, plaster and bricks had already begun flaking off the dome. In a few years the minarets, the stone columns of the cupola galleries, and the vaults of the portals and outer domes had all collapsed.

In 1399, after Timur returned from his successful campaign in India with booty and craftsmen, he decided to rebuild Samarkand's congregational mosque in honor of his senior consort, Saray Mulk Khanum. The huge edifice covered an area measuring 548 × 357.5 feet. The mosque followed the traditional Persian four-*iwan* plan. (An *iwan* is a vaulted hall open at one end.) In the late 1970s the Soviets began restoring the Bibi Khanum mosque. Here the sanctuary *iwan* is seen under scaffolding.

The desire to build such a lofty structure resulted in the collapse of the main prayer hall and its huge dome not long after its completion. Using the excuse of excessive spending, Timur had the two architects, Khwaja Mahmud Davud and Mohammed-Jald, executed in 1404. Like the palace of Aq Sarai in Shahr-i-Sabz, the Bibi Khanum has tremendous pylons, one of which is under restoration here. The use of *banai* decoration is very successful.

By way of explanation the story is told of Timur's Persian architect insisting on a kiss from Saray Mulk herself as his price for finishing the work before her husband's return. She, of course, refused. But when word reached her that Timur was in Merv, no more than a week's march away, she decided to allow the architect to kiss her cheek through her veil. Unfortunately, the Persian's kiss burned such a hole that a black spot appeared on her skin. To hide it the Princess had herself and her entire court attired in veils. When Timur found out the truth he had her burned at the stake. Meanwhile Timur's men pursued the architect up to the top of the dome where, it is said, wings suddenly sprouted out of his shoulders and off he flew to Mashhad.

Some buildings may look better as ruins than they ever did intact, and Gippenreiter has a photograph of the Bibi Khanum's dome taken before the 1975 restoration that shows it in its original colors, complete with the most poetic of cracks. But the project of rebuilding a structure of the Bibi Khanum's scale could not help but appeal to the men in the Kremlin and, over local protests—this isn't restoration, it's invention—this elephant has been allowed to add a new blue of its own to the Samarkand skyline.

The dome of the Bibi Khanum mosque overlooks the Samarkand bazaar, just as it has for the past 600 years.

Timur's heir and favorite grandson, Mohammed Sultan, died in battle in 1402. The grieving ruler returned his grandson's body to Samarkand and ordered the construction of a mausoleum next to the madrasah commissioned by Mohammed Sultan. Later this mausoleum became Timur's own tomb and that of his heirs. The complex of buildings known as Gur Emir consisted of the mausoleum, the madrasah, a khanaqah, and numerous chambers. The octagonal mausoleum is topped by a fluted, melon-shaped double dome. Tiled in a brilliant cobalt blue, the dome is 112 feet high. The monumental entranceway, exquisitely decorated in mosaic faience, was commissioned by Ulugh Beg in 1434 and bears the inscription of the craftsman, Mohammed b. Mahmud al-Isfahani.

The Gur Emir Mausoleum

The soaring cupola of the Gur Emir mausoleum is covered in brilliant gold leaf and lapis blue. This photo was taken after the recent restoration.

By the time Timur commissions the Gur Emir, the "King's Grave," ostensibly for a favorite grandson and heir apparent, but in fact for himself—these are not matters you leave to others—the circumstances of his regime and, one must suppose, of his personal tastes have changed; nothing less than jewelry will do. The inside wall panel (up to waist height) is a warm yellowish-green onyx marble. The perforated railing around the tomb site is alabaster. The slab covering Timur's own grave is a single piece of nephrite jade somehow brought back from Khotan. There is even a white circular rug, still extant only seventy years ago, its design of arabesques and flowers woven into a perfectly matched white background, with a space in the middle for the green-veined tombstone.

Such ostentation usually affronts. But Timur carries it off, and with its flower-tiled walls, its airy lavender and gold ceiling twinkling like the eye of a great sunflower, and its uniquely tapering melon dome, the mausoleum is all of a piece in a way few memorials are. It adds up to nothing less than a vision of paradise. And in the surrounding accompaniments—the entombed mullah at whose feet he has chosen to lie, the inscription chiseled over his tomb, "If I were alive people would not be glad"—we feel the presence of a man who has taken the measure of himself and has no regrets.

The good luck that allowed Timur to fight to such a ripe old age has continued to preserve him even in death. Other graves get robbed, but when the Persian conqueror Nadir Shah tries to prize off Timur's burial slab he is forced to give up after cracking it in two. The Soviets of the Stalin era are less superstitious. They have a life-size statue that they want to honor him with, and on June 21, 1941 they haul him out of his grave and find that he was indeed red bearded, at 5' 8" of above average height for a Tatar, and lame in his right arm and leg. It is no accident, the Uzbeks believe, that this is the very day his modern successor, Hitler, chooses to invade the Soviet Union.

EARLY TWENTIETH-CENTURY PHOTOGRAPHS OF SAMARKAND AND BUKHARA

Above: This traditionally turbaned mullah, standing before the intricately carved doors of the Gur Emir, is the guardian of the mausoleum.

Left: The Gur Emir, with the walls of the adjacent khanaqah and madrasah still intact. The high drum of the dome is covered with *banai* Kufic inscription.

PAGE 60
Detail of the ornamentation in the Gur Emir. The geometric design forms duodecagonal and pentagonal stars and rhomboid shapes in stucco and gold leaf. Within the rhomboids, Kufic inscriptions repeat the name of the Prophet Mohammed three times.

The Shah-e-Zindeh. In the fore-ground is the summer mosque (left) and the entrance to the Dawlat Kushbegi madrasah (right). Mullahs in turbans and colorful dress were once guardians of the mausoleums. The mausoleum of Tughlu Tekin is seen in its ruinous state beyond the second *chahartaq* at the top of the hill.

PAGE 63
Top: Even in ruins, the Bibi Kha-num mosque towers majestically over the makeshift stalls of the Sam-arkand bazaar. Its huge portal arch measures 60 feet wide and 130 feet high.

Bottom: The Shah-e-Zindeh build-ings are located on a hilly outcrop to the north of Samarkand, offering a dramatic view of the ruins of the Bibi Khanum mosque.

PAGES **64–65**, CLOCKWISE FROM TOP LEFT:
   A group of Sarts enjoying their tea and waterpipe in front of a mosque.

   The terrace of a house is the setting for eating the traditional rice dish, pelao. Using hands or bread, not cutlery, is the rule.

   A Tajik woman playing the dutar, an ancient, two-stringed folk instrument.

   A Sart's reclining couch *(takht)* is not only a comfortable resting place but a symbol of leisure.

   Painted dancing boys *(batcha)* performed sinuous dances to the accompaniment of tambourines and bangles.

   The teahouse overlooking the Samarkand grain market. Bird cages hang in the trees.

Neatly wrapped cones of tobacco advertise this merchant's specialty.

A melon merchant at a bazaar in Bukhara. The huge melons, carefully stored, could be kept for months, from harvest until mid-winter.

The cobbled streets and makeshift awnings of this early twentieth-century bazaar in Bukhara are rarely seen today.

A fruit merchant in Bukhara. The decorated pans overhead may have been used for measuring produce.

In Afrasiab, on the outskirts of ancient Samarkand, hundreds of Sarts on horseback en-
gage in a fierce game of *buzkashi*, played with
a severed sheep's head instead of a ball.

PAGE 69
Top left: A young Tajik woman from
Samarkand, richly attired in a fur-lined
winter robe, an elaborate gold diadem, and
gold earrings.

Bottom left: The tunic worn by this Tajik
from Bukhara clearly shows the origins of the
paisley design that has now spread throughout the world.

Right: Beneath her silk-lined robe (*shubas* or
khalat), this young Tajik woman wears several layers of garments over a cotton dress.

Sarts heading for the madrasahs in the Registan, Samarkand's central square. The domes and minarets of the madrasahs can be seen in the distance.

The courtyard of the Shir Dar madrasah in the Registan. The two-story gallery of individual cells functioned as student dormitories or classrooms.

Without money changers, the complex trade network would have broken down. An abacus was essential for computing the transactions.

The inner courtyard of the Tilla Kari madrasah in the Registan. The madrasah was built to function both as a theological school and as a congregational mosque. Here the faithful are performing their Friday prayers. Today the Tilla Kari is no longer used for its original functions.

The observatory of Ulugh Beg (fifteenth century) confirms the role of Samarkand as a major artistic and scientific center. It was rediscovered in 1908 by the Russian archeologist Vyatkin. The circular three-story structure housed a curved trench with steps that marked off degrees. Astronomers were able to determine the angular positions of stars and planets by the light they cast on this trench through an opening in the observatory.

PAGES 74–75
Registan means "sandy marketplace." In 1417 Ulugh Beg, then governor of Samarkand, ordered the construction of a madrasah and other structures in the Registan. In the seventeenth century the Shaybanid khans followed the plan of Ulugh Beg's madrasah and constructed the Shir Dar madrasah directly across from it. The Tilla Kari madrasah was then built in between these two structures.

The Registan

Timur's own successor in Samarkand was his grandson Ulugh Beg, the only son of Shah Rukh and Robert Byron's heroine Gohar Shad. Ulugh Beg was a great astronomer. His calculations of the earth's calendar, made from data gathered in his impressive observatory, are only

The courtyard of the Ulugh Beg madrasah. Constructed in 1417–20 according to the four-*iwan* plan, the madrasah was originally flanked by a mosque and a khanaqah. Today only the madrasah remains. Its mosaic faience and *banai* technique are of exceptional quality. Two minarets flank the entrance *pishtaq*, the high façade of which is seen here. The cells for students repeat the ogival pattern of the four principal *iwans*. The tree in the center of the courtyard provides shade.

six hours off. As a ruler Ulugh Beg wanted to make Samarkand the center of the new enlightenment. To attract the intellectuals he builds a religious academy (1417–20) in the middle of the Registan that is intended to outshine anything in Central Asia. Whereas another's investment in "plant" might include a gymnasium or a great swimming pool, he goes in for tile—acres of it. The success is such that two more madrasahs in even more wondrous tile are built on the square in the seventeenth century, the Shir Dar (1619–36) and the Tilla Kari (1646–60). What one feels about all this oversized neo-Persian architecture, isolated from the street life that once made the Registan teem like a

Detail of the mosaic faience in the courtyard of the Ulugh Beg madrasah. To make mosaic faience the craftsman first fires tiles in different colors, then cuts them into the necessary shapes to form the desired panel. The technique is difficult, extremely labor intensive, and therefore expensive, but creates faience of exceptional quality and lasting brilliance. The duodecagonal-petalled flower pattern is placed within a twelve-sided star that radiates out, forming various geometric shapes.

The Kufic inscriptions on the Shir Dar *pishtaq*, with its famous lion and sun images, are exemplary of sixteenth-century *banai* technique. They include the *shahada*, the proclamation of faith. The attached corner columns also have inscriptions inset in geometric patterns. In *Turkestan Solo*, Ella Maillart wrote of the Shir Dar, "The architect has built the arch of this portal with such perfection that the entire heavens gnaws its fingers in astonishment, thinking it sees the rising of some new moon."

second Piazza di San Marco, is open to question. But the acoustics of this naturally echoing space with its great portals and recessed arches do make for an unrivaled concert hall.

It may be argued that the artistic achievements of the Timurid dynasty lie not in Samarkand but further afield—in the great buildings Gohar Shad was to erect in Mashhad and Herat, the Herat school of miniature painting, and the Moghul art of Northern India. But theater on the civic scale of a Samarkand is a rather impure form of art. We judge it not as much by what it is in itself as by its impact, the energy waves it sends out; its ability, in short, to keep us sitting there, en-

Detail of the dome and top of the minaret of Shir Dar. The ribbed dome has a *muqarnas* (stalactite) border, below which is an inscription from the Koran in *thulth* script. The minaret has Kufic inscriptions. Maillart wrote, "Only the eagle of thought could presume to attain to the summit of this medersa [sic]," and, "Never, in all the centuries will an acrobat's thought, even with the bow of phantasy, scale the forbidden heights of this minaret."

The last madrasah in the Registan is the Tilla Kari (gold work). Situated at the north end of the square, in between the Ulugh Beg and Shir Dar madrasahs, it was commissioned by Yalangtush Bahadur in 1646 to function both as a madrasah and as a congregational mosque. Its exterior is magnificently decorated, as this detail of the façade reveals. Insets of mosaic faience, *banai* technique, and underglaze painted tile are used for the revetment of the façade. On the attached spiral corner columns are small inscriptions that read: "May the end be well" and "Glory be to God, and praise be to God."

Interior of the *muqarnas* cupola of the Tilla
Kari madrasah after restoration. The transition from the square walls to the dome is
achieved by means of squinches that are covered in *muqarnas* decoration. The ornate gold
and lapis stucco of the interior received a new
coat of gold leaf during restoration.

Detail of the corner
squinches that ascend to
the cupola, with their
stellar inlays and painted
ornaments. A band of in-
scription defines the zone
of transition from the
walls to the dome.

Detail of the *mihrab* in the Tilla Kari madrasah. The *mihrab* is the niche that indicates the *qibla,* or direction of Mecca, toward which Muslims pray.

thralled, night after night, year after year. That Timur's theater could go on playing for the next couple of centuries in Bukhara and was still running strong in Khiva some four hundred years later says a lot for the quality of the energy he generated.

Daily Life

Everyone I meet keeps pointing to Afghanistan and wringing their hands. They all acknowledge that the invasion was a mistake. The same could be said about the Russian annexation of Turkestan, and I was prepared to say it. But communism has fallen on fertile soil here. The Russians have just celebrated their millennium as a Christian nation. Samarkand for its part celebrated its 2,500th anniversary in 1970. Having to cope all that time with the whims of Greeks, Arabs, Persians, Mongols, Uzbeks, and now Russians has created a highly civilized people, perfectly adapted to the complexities of modern life. In Moscow the disruption caused by the revolution has been such that even today very little works. The nearest shopping center is, as they say, seven thousand miles away. In Samarkand, however, everything works, even, one may hazard, communism. One can see why vacationing Russians might well prefer it to the resorts of the Crimea. It would be hard to imagine a more pleasant city in which to develop a tan.

In my case this concept took a while to sink in. There was so much that was new that my first days were largely taken up with trying to view the monuments in their various lights and going on excursions: to Timur's birthplace at Shahr-i-Sabz; to the new shrine of Ismail al-Bokhari; or to one or another eye-opening collective farm. There is nothing wrong with such traipsing about; an oasis is all that surrounds it. And you may have to wait for a vocabulary to develop before you can think of sitting down somewhere and letting a bazaar's faces, costumes, be theater enough.

As you sit there on a terrace overlooking the comings and goings of the market, you find yourself taking in a tempo. Slow, slower, slowest might well define it, one round-bodied Sart after another stopping, pausing, as he makes his rounds. The hills, the fierceness of the noon sun, have much to do with it. You don't stir unless you can feel a bit of breeze. If there is none you sit down and order a pot of tea or duck into a bathhouse. When you emerge you can be sure the wind will have started up, a whole gladness filling your pores as you walk.

This tempo is not entirely your illusion. You have only to observe the traffic. In other cities you know how it proceeds, honking, swearing,

To this day the bazaar in Samarkand is a festive and crowded place. In the past, goods from East and West were traded here; nineteenth-century travelers noted that Tuesdays and Sundays were the best days for going to market.

PAGE 85
The famous Turkmen rugs, with their brilliant colors and distinctive designs, are for sale at the bazaars.

Their clothes may be traditional, but these women are breaking with the past, when only men sold goods at the bazaar.

shaking its fists. Here there's not a car or a motorcycle that would think of advancing at anything above a crawl. The streets, they know, do not belong to them.

In the old days domestic life went on behind the blue-painted doorways, in the secluded fastness of a courtyard. Nowadays the courtyards are mostly deserted. All you find in them is the family car and some lines of drying laundry. The rest of life has moved out onto the street. And it is here that you find people of an evening, propped on benches against a compound wall or squatting on their heels in a wire-enclosed weed patch, observing the passersby, the whirligig of children's games.

This may sound as if life is a question of *dolce far niente*. On the contrary, people work very hard, and with the help of the labor pool provided by their large, highly educated families, Uzbekistan is as productive as any republic in the Soviet Union. But for the Sart, work is only a means to an end, and that end is abundance. The Sart wants to be surrounded—by children, by his own often vast girth. He can't go anywhere without eating something, nuts, a cone of sunflower seeds, a sherbet. The restaurant plates may be small, but every square inch is stacked like a child's tower. Nor is there anything distanced, finicky, in his greetings. The whole face lights up at the sight of a friend. It is returned, vividly. Then they clasp each other warmly by the shoulders.

The notion of families with an average of twelve children would have most of us throwing up our hands in dismay. A surer recipe for continuing poverty and ecological disaster is hard to imagine. But in a well-educated community where everyone works hard, it makes for an enviable dynamism. There are people around, and as in Japan, the numbers allow you to plan. In a time of chaos, of a wholesale shift in values, they also insulate you. As for the trouble of raising so many children, the Sarts claim that it's not the large families that take up your time, but the middle-size ones. Large families run themselves. And the children don't move away when they grow up. When building a house a farmer makes sure that there is enough space for his children to have houses of their own. A Russian is perfectly happy to move for the sake of a better job. A Sart, never.

With this vast sustaining envelope around him it is not surprising that the Sart should have such a sense of measure, appropriateness, calm. None of the hysterical shouting that so many of us indulge in. If you do hear someone shrieking in a corridor or see someone throwing a punch in a kvass line, you can bet it's a Russian.

The scale of things in Samarkand is as notoriously grand as in Moscow: 30,000-person collective farms; giant hotels like the one I'm staying in. But it works here because everyone is so organized. In the hotel restaurant the courses appear one after another. Within a few hours the space will have changed from a folk dance theater to a restaurant to a roaring, vodka-besotted, old-fashioned ocean-liner dance hall. If the restaurant can only seat you in ten minutes, that's that, you think. But if you are not there a quarter of an hour later, here is the waiter out in the hall very kindly, you feel, looking for you.

On a farm, extra labor is never brought in for a harvest. And, despite the lack of machines, the work gets done because the supervisor and his staff are always meeting. You see them gathering after dinner, at eight in the evening, to plan the next day's deployment to the last man-hour.

At the heart of the system is a degree of choice. No one is coerced to work where he does. The factories, the collective farms, have to compete for workers, offer them nurseries, schools, housing, saunas. The worker is in this sense the consumer. The better the work goes, the more everyone benefits.

Time for your family? Well, there are weekends. Not that work ceases, but you can work together, on your family plot, in your own time. And if selling at the bazaar is somewhat hazardous, it does at least get you there, into that eye-opening bewilderment.

We are accustomed to hearing how farmers glory in their independence; they would not want it any other way. But you notice that they complain a lot about the daily enormity, about the twelve- to sixteen-hour days that await them. Mortgaged to the hilt as they are, they have to work such long hours or be ruined. And they visibly carry this accumulation of worry on their deeply creased, weather-beaten faces.

The Sart, however, is never obliged to burden himself with such headaches as gambling on the market or growing crops that will only be destroyed. He has time. If he wants to progress there are schools where he can specialize, study agronomy, learn machine repair. He is not always laboring in solitude at tasks below his mental capacities.

This does not mean that life on a collective farm is not without its occasional scandal. When I arrived a trial was being prepared in Moscow for the Uzbekistan Party officials who had invented a whole series of cotton fields, swindling the nation out of some three billion rubles over a number of years. And I was shown stocks of lethal chemicals that had been distributed to the collective farms before they had been sufficiently tested. I was also able to see how a campaign as necessary as the one against alcohol could be interpreted in such a way that the growing of wine-producing grapes that might have allowed the Soviet Union to earn foreign currency was drastically curtailed. Faced with having to uproot his 2,500-year-old grape stocks, one

Baked goods sell quickly at
the Samarkand bazaar . . .

. . . perhaps because they are
so appetizingly displayed.

manager of a Georgian collective felt he had no choice but to take his life—an event that shocked even Moscow.

Looking for a Wedding

A Moscow friend says that you can always tell the soul of a country by its poetry. Or if it's the art of happiness that interests you, its music will do, the social music occasioned, say, by a wedding. The hard part, of course, is finding it. But once you have thrust your foreign face through the gateway, everything is taken care of. In Samarkand the families are large enough so that you can usually count on finding one, and I have known vacationing students who have kept themselves fed by going from one to the next for months.

One evening the folk dance troupe in my hotel devoted the second half of its program to rendering a "typical" wedding for us tourists. With its utterly veiled bride, costumed dancers, and beautifully played, highly dissonant music, it was good enough to whet my appetite for the real thing.

I wasn't up to hanging out by the Lenin memorial to wait for the wreath layers to come by fresh from the Registry Office. And on foot I couldn't keep the honking cars in sight long enough to pin down exactly where they were headed.

Fortunately my last evening in Samarkand is not only a Saturday, but the eve of Ramadan, the month-long Muslim fast. If anything is going on, it will be this evening, I figure, so I strike out through the warren of alleys behind the Gur Emir mausoleum.

I have been walking for some time when I pass a festively dressed house. There is a carpet slung over the wall as if by way of announcement and a line of men sitting on chairs outside the main door. Across the street many women can be seen inside a doorway, and on both sides of the street there is evidence of food, cakes, and other sweets piled high on a courtyard table. It seems to be exactly what I am looking for.

I go on a little farther until, at the corner of the house, just out of sight, a group of young men hail me and motion me to sit down. Willingly I accept; it's a pleasure on such a lovely evening to sit with people. They have a teapot they have been passing among themselves, would I like some? Certainly, I reply. And in a little while a teapot arrives for me, just for me, it is solemnly explained, along with a dish of almond cookies and turnovers. The sweets are stacked one on top of another, with that overwhelming generosity you encounter time and again. Soon another dish, of meat samsas, is brought. All this sits before me on a chair and, while I take up another chair, my hosts are obliged to display the art of sharing space, two to a seat. In sign language I ask whether this is a wedding. No, they say, the party after a funeral.

By now the sight of all this food being spirited my way has attracted the principal mourner, a handsome, confident-looking cybernetics professor in the university mathematics department. It is his father, a top judge in Tashkent, he tells me in surprising English, who has died at the age of sixty-four.

Before we can talk further he is called away to greet a new arrival, leaving us to pick up as best we can. The talking is not exactly easy. On my side I possess perhaps a half dozen words of Persian, learned half a lifetime ago. Two of them have a smidgen of English learned at school, the others a few names plucked from the newspapers. Nevertheless, for much of two hours we go on, reaching as far as we can into our memory banks and pulling out the various loaves and fishes: Gorbachev, Reagan, *perestroika,* Muhammad Ali, Angela Davis, Platini, Wilt Chamberlain. Finally, every last word milked, I rise to my feet, and you can see from their faces how relieved the whole company is. They have passed a real test, but oh, how hard it has been.

It is quite dark now as I start back to my hotel. I have gone little more than a couple of blocks when I hear the strains of a wedding band. In the middle of a lane cordoned off by an eye-level piece of green plastic, an accordion and clarinet are playing before several long tables of diners. The music, moreover, is what I like best, twirling *karsilimas* dances in a sprightly seven-eighths rhythm, two-steps like ''Doctor, Doctor.'' And I must say I am sorely tempted. But instead of linking the songs together, medley style, the musicians stop after each one, with the result that the momentum needed to propel me through the gates is lacking. And it is this that finally permits me, after some twenty minutes, to tear myself away. This, and my perception that the evening, in the persons of the young men I had been sitting with, has already happened. There is such a thing as enough, and at that moment, I know, I have struck it. All I want now is to walk back to my hotel while I can still retain everything: the skullcaps and arched eyebrows of the youths squeezed onto their few chairs all around me, that magicianlike, one-rabbit-after-the-next-pulled-out-of-the-hat hospitality.

Above: The flora and fauna peculiar to the Kara Kum desert are protected in the Badkhyz Preserve in Soviet Turkmenia. The Horsfields terrapin *(Testudo horsfield)* thrives in the semidesert terrain.

Right: Fields of poppies, once harvested for the Chinese opium market, cover the Kara Kum in spring.

PAGE 93
Desert blooms.

PAGES 94–95
The saksaul tree *(haloxylon)* is native to the semidesert and desert areas of Central Asia. It reaches a height of twenty to thirty feet and has a lifespan of thirty to sixty years. Its thick, contorted branches sprout grayish leaves and pink fruit. The saksaul's hard and brittle wood is used for firewood and its green branchlets serve as winter fodder for camels and sheep.

An apricot *(orik)* tree in full bloom. Apricots are a favored fruit and dried apricots are sold year round at the bazaar.

The delicate flowers of the *alycha,* a kind of Damson plum tree, another common fruit tree in Central Asia.

✾ BUKHARA ✾

Bukhara lies some four hundred kilometers west of Samarkand and five hundred meters lower. Nearing it, the Zerafshan River, now little more than a trickle, takes one last look, throws up its hands, and dives into the earth, never to reappear. Ten kilometers to the other side the Kyzyl Kum desert begins and stretches as far as Khwarezm, a crossing of two nights and a day by train. Whereas Samarkand's soil is a yellow-brown loess, Bukhara's is an alkaline gray so drenched in salt that only 10 percent is arable. The only way to grow anything is to irrigate. But irrigation has its problems, as you have to get rid of the salt that builds up. Before planting cotton, the dominant crop to an even greater extent than around Samarkand, the fields must be washed anywhere from two to twenty times. They are then sprayed with weed killer. Add the defoliants that must be used if the cotton is to be picked by machine and you grasp why the only place you see birds in any abundance is out at the edge of the desert. The symbol of Bukhara, the stork—their nests once occupied every minaret—hasn't been seen since 1974.

Not set on a great caravan crossroads as Samarkand is, Bukhara has always had to rely on the products of its hands and brains to survive. In the Middle Ages the reputation of its learning was such—Muslims are, after all, the People of the Book—that students were drawn to it from all over the Muslim world. As Fitzroy Maclean notes, "Elsewhere in the world light came down from heaven; but from Bukhara it went up." It may even be this intellectual tradition that helped persuade the Uzbeks when they came to power in the late sixteenth century to make Bukhara, and not Samarkand, the regional capital, a position it would hold until 1917. It is this region, which extends to the Afghan border, and not the city, that gave its name to the famous carpets.

Of this heritage a great deal survives. Bukhara's soil may not be as fertile as that of Samarkand and Khiva, but buildings stay up in it, and some twenty are genuine masterpieces, ranging in time from the exquisite ninth-century Samanid mausoleum to the early twentieth-century Bala Hauz and emir's Summer Palace.

Beyond this array of architecture is the living expanse of the old mud-walled town, hardly changed in the last four hundred years. The windowless, thick-walled houses with their jutting, riflelike wooden beams may lack most modern amenities, but they are well insulated, and the inhabitants prefer the inconvenience to the terror of living suspended in space in an earthquake-prone apartment block.

Thrust into this seething labyrinth, your first impression may well be one of intense elation. It is hard not to believe that here at last your journey is snapping into focus.

In Samarkand your expectations have to make all sorts of accommodations. Here, under a sky of a blue such as you have never beheld,

Like many Islamic cities, Bukhara was originally surrounded by a rampart built of unbaked clay. Now in ruins, this rampart dates back to the time of the Turkish emirate in the eighteenth century.

PAGE 98
The Kalyan mosque (1514), the congregational mosque of Bukhara, is said to hold 120,000 worshippers. Pictured here is the sanctuary *iwan*, in front of which is an octagonal ablution fountain *(Taratkhaneh)*. The sanctuary *iwan* indicates the direction of Mecca; its *pishtaq* and dome are taller than those of the other three *iwans*.

Domes of the bazaar of the money changers *(taq Sarafan)* in Bukhara. The Persian word for vault, *taq*, has become synonymous with bazaar, because of the vaulted form of the covered bazaar's roofs.

against a background of mud, with dresses, robes, caps, and turbans jumping out at you, everything looks right. And you can't help but rejoice that the time clocks of history haven't been taken out of their faces and smashed on the ground.

At the same time you recognize what someone must feel who has dropped into an Andean forest without a bird guide. Everything is flashing—mud, brick, tile, minarets, domes—but the whole process of finding your way around takes precedence over putting a name on what you are seeing, let alone guessing what it all means.

This getting around, as in any labyrinth, is not easy. You have a destination, the Tower of Death, blasting forth its twelfth-century phallic beacon some twenty-five minutes away at the ancient end of the city. But between you and it, every few hundred yards, loom four bazaars. With their overlapping turtle-dome roofs—wonderful jungle gyms for the children!—the bazaars are justly famous seventeeth-century creations. But as pedestrian rotaries they leave a lot to be desired. Every time you enter one you are spun around, because you don't exit on the same axis as you have entered. A couple of them and you are utterly lost, and chances are you are fuming.

What holds for getting around applies in a different way to the Bukhara equivalents of the Registan and the Bibi Khanum that you

The vaulted covered bazaar is a common feature in Islamic cities. It provides shade and a controlled climate year round.

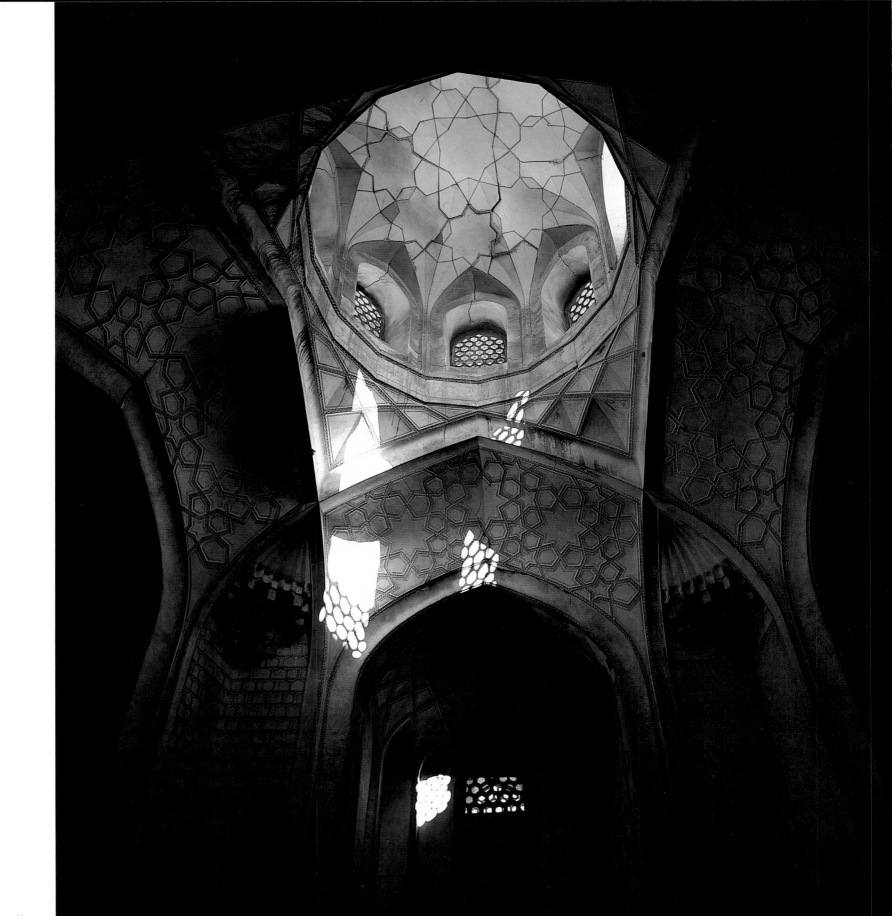

happen to blunder upon. You can see that you are being confronted with what Gippenreiter calls another form of perspective, something quite different from the eye-level viewpoint bequeathed to us by the Renaissance. But to free it from this sense of what it isn't and make it flash—bird, word, flight, space—is not a change a Western-trained pair of eyes can achieve all that readily. (Art Nouveau latched on well enough to the aspect of pattern, but it never had the craftsmen to elaborate the sculptured walls that turn a room into a piece of music.)

Then one evening at my hotel, as I am watching a pre-wedding dance—arms, hands, even fingers gracefully weaving, conjuring holes and vortices, smoke circles drifting away like notes—it occurs to me that the gestures I am seeing are akin to those I have been staring at all afternoon on one or another abstractly carved door. I can even think of certain turn-of-the-century composers—Ravel, Debussy, Albeniz at the end of his life—who captured something of these weaving hands, these percussive castanet-like interventions. All through Islamic culture there is the same projection of a world seen in certain conditions as garden, as joy.

What are these conditions? Well, it may be helpful to start with where I am sitting if I am so lucky as to find myself in that illuminated page of a finished Central Asian room. No, not erect in a chair. Not squatting on my heels, effortlessly balanced, either—a feat, alas, quite beyond me. Rather I am sprawled on my back and elbows in a corner, as one might take tea on the floor of a tent. What first draws my eye is the point farthest away, infinity realized, pouring down from its painted ceiling, its mausoleum dome: fireworks, a starry sky; yes, God has many names. But it is this distance and the power gathered into all the intervening space that so attracts. For this reason the spaces are not the body-sized ones of a Western home, the ceiling hardly higher than we can reach with a hammer standing on a chair, the paintings hung at eye level. Instead, the ornamentation is all up there, Tiepolo-like, but we are not lying in bed looking up at it, at those rosy nymphs and sporting satyrs, we are sprawled in the dust.

Sprawled there a notion occurs: if there is an ecstatic point from which a dome's ornament radiates down, might there not be a visual progression gradually intensifying as it ascends? Look at the brickwork patterns of a minaret, exactly where the galleries start to break out, to flower. Or notice how everything in a room goes berserk as you approach the upper corners: stalactite grottos; magnificently orchestrated geometric fountains; the color glowing positively dizzyingly between the ceiling beams, one glorious riff after the next carved out in Allah's favor. Lastly, notice the walls themselves, the extent to which a flat surface has been set vibrating with perforations, niches, alcoves, and

Interior of the mosque of the Abdullah Khan madrasah (1588–90) in Bukhara. Unusual fan-shaped vaulting, ornamented with *muqarnas*, forms the transition to the dome. The latticed windows *(panjara)* around the central dome diffuse the light coming into the mosque.

103

Interior of the winter mosque of the Abdulaziz Khan madrasah (1651–52), Bukhara. The unusually complex geometric patterns of the ornately patterned *muqarnas* make this building unique.

Detail of the vaulting in the summer mosque of the Abdulaziz Khan madrasah (1651–52). The floral and other natural motifs, painted in deep gold, blue, and white, form complex geometric patterns.

Detail of the dome of the Khwaja Zainud-Din mosque-khanaqah (sixteenth century), Bukhara. The ribbed dome, with its elaborate *muqarnas* ornamentation, rests on alternating squinches and arches.

mirrored recesses. Behind it all lies an energy intent on conjuring up orifices of every conceivable variety and not in the least put off by the scale of what may be no more than a student's humble cell.

The amount of labor required for such perfection might strike us as excessive. How could one ever be expected to finish a whole house! But that's just the point. In the whole of a madrasah one may find only one decorated room. If someone else comes along and wants to restore his room, so much the better, but it's not what you expect. That's why, even in palaces that are still in use, beautifully painted rooms and utter ruins often exist within a few feet of one another without anyone seeming the least embarrassed.

As to what fueled all these curves, this restlessness of design, one can only speculate. Michaux says somewhere that there is no prevision for any of this labyrinthine architecture in the Koran. Marijuana? Opium? Then again Michaux may be wrong to want billiard-ball causality to come popping out of the Koranic text. One eminent scholar, Michael Beard, believes that this phenomenon might be explained by the bouncing antinarrative quality of the Koran in combination with forms inherited from Byzantine architecture.

Left: Detail of a niche in the Khwaja Zainud-Din. The entire surface is painted, including cells of the *muqarnas*, creating a rich, carpet-like effect.

Right: Detail of the interior of the Khwaja Zainud-Din. The lower section of the walls is covered with tilework. The border, with its running floral motif, frames a geometric configuration of hexagonal tiles.

107

Completed before 907, the Mausoleum of Ismail the Samanid in Bukhara is one of the most impressive structures of early Islamic architecture. It attests to the potential of brick as both a building and a decorative material. Brick beading frames the four doorways, and diagonally set endbricks form a dogtooth pattern in the spandrels.

PAGE 109
This ingenious cubical mausoleum looks monumental but measures only thirty-one feet on each side. Its corner columns, each topped by a little dome, buttress the tapering walls. The open arcade below the cornice forms an inner gallery. Like wickerwork (*hezarbaf*—literally, a thousand interweavings), the texture and design of the brick create playful effects of light and shade.

The Samanid Mausoleum

Cultural historians are wont to talk as if there is such a thing as progression in art. I am struck, on the contrary, by how often the work that announces a new direction is never surpassed. What holds for Homer, or the novel of Cervantes, Fielding, Laclos, and Stendhal, holds for the Samanid mausoleum. Built by the Persian-speaking ruler Ismail sometime before A.D. 907, it marks not only the first use of baked bricks and the first mausoleum in Central Asia but must rank with Isfahan's Friday mosque as one of the most beautiful brick buildings ever built.

The mausoleum is small, measuring no more than thirty-one feet on each of its four sides. But the slightly swollen adobe base on which it stands and the way the corner columns, set off by a wedge of shadow, lean in, narrowing as they rise (making the top gallery, with its row of arches and tiny zigzag columns, appear to bulge out) create the illusion of something almost monumental. When combined with the rhythms of the brick, the jutting knobs, the perforated repetitions—diamonds, wheels, punctured honeycombs—the effect is that of an intensely layered percussive symphony. It dances, reverberates out at you from all sides, in every timbre of voice, and the more you walk around it the more aware you become of the rhythmic clapping, the shouting out in joy, of a whole singularly patterned world; one, moreover, that, because of the different clays used in the dome, changes with each hour of the day, becoming, as all commentators agree, most vibrant at night.

Even today the people still place candles in the holes and niches to bring out the percussive effects and carry questions and poems written out on scraps of paper into the tomb proper to be illuminated. Similar feelings of veneration must have inspired the people in the days preceding the Mongol invasion, when they decided to bury the mosque rather than see it razed. There it remained, indistinguishable under its mound from the adjoining cemetery, until a Bolshevik soldier with a pitchfork happened onto it. It's hard to think of one of the world's great buildings vanishing into a seven-hundred-year hole in the ground, harder still to imagine it emerging from its deep sleep looking so very youthful and mysterious.

The interior brickwork of the Samanid mausoleum is similar to that of the exterior. The use of squinches in the zone of transition from the square chamber to the low hemispherical dome was an innovation. The squinches assured the stability of the dome.

The Kalyan Minar, one of the earliest and most outstanding monuments in Central Asia, is a tall, tapering minaret 164 feet high. Built in 1127, it was part of a congregational mosque that is no longer extant. Like the Samanid mausoleum, it exemplifies the virtuosity of the brick mason. Horizontal bands of wickerwork *(hezarbaf)* brick design and inscription ring the tower. The monotony of the buff-colored brick is broken by one band of turquoise glazed tiles. From the gallery at the top, the muezzin would call out the prayer five times each day. The cornice is covered with *muqarnas* decoration.

The Tower of Death

From the twelfth century onward the heart of Bukhara has been the Kalyan Minar, or the Tower of Death as it is customarily known. One would expect a building of its height to have long since collapsed. But minarets, by virtue of their conical design, ride out the seismic shocks better than most structures, and the Tower of Death was built to last. To ensure that the composition of sand and clay out of which the bricks were cast was resistant enough, the overseer would bury ten coins in each mound. The mounds were then pounded until the last coin was struck. When the bricks were finally sunbaked they were laid out in a long row and the overseer galloped his horse over them. If any splintered the whole lot had to be redone. Not long ago a rock

Framing the magnificent Kalyan Minar are the Kalyan mosque (1512–39) on the right, which replaced the original twelfth-century congregational mosque, and the Mir Arab madrasah (1530s) on the left.

The twelfth-century Mughak-i Attari (Apothecaries) mosque is the oldest surviving mosque in Bukhara. It is exemplary of a neighborhood mosque. Long neglected, it has sunken some fifteen feet below street level. Like the Kalyan Minar, its brickwork is both functional and decorative. The monotone color of the brick is relieved by the insertion of terra-cotta panels.

Facade of the Mughak-i Attari mosque. Here decorative terra-cotta panels frame the doorway.

The Chashma Ayub, or Job's well, is a monument to the spring that the prophet is reputed to have set flowing. In close proximity to the Samanid mausoleum, it was erected in the twelfth century and reworked in the 1380s. Above the central nave are three cupolas. Directly over the site of the well is a short tower capped by a conical roof.

climber gave them his own twentieth-century testing. The tower may not be Everest, but it is all the same an impressive ascent.

The Royal Dungeons

A stone's throw from the Tower of Death lie the infamous royal dungeons, now converted into the Soviet equivalent of a Mme. Tussaud's. Why Westerners fail to visit them is hard to say, but at virtually any hour of the day one can come upon several busloads of awestruck Soviet tourists peering down into the well-like depths. Here and there for purposes of greater realism a wall has been cut away and artificially lit so that one can take in the lifelike exhibits of poor wretches bent over or crawling listlessly about, chained by one of a variety of shackles: manacles, ankle chains, neck collars linked to a wall peg by a twenty-foot chain. These oubliettes were so deep that the prisoner had to be lowered in by rope. There, in what amounted to a zoo cage, he languished, surviving the attentions of the specially bred, three-inch-long tarantulas and sharing with his fellow prisoners whatever food happened to be flung down, until such time as the emir "should deign to remember him."

The Bala Hauz Mosque

The twentieth century has come around. You have already erected every conceivable type of mosque, from the sixteenth-century Namazgah, big enough to accommodate the region's entire male population (outside the walls, of course, and used but twice a year), to tiny ones like the four-turreted Char Minar (1807), seemingly built for nothing more than to house a library and a pair of storks—with what are you now going to amaze God? You have a certain folk craftsman, Shirin Muradov, who wants to build you a summer palace five miles outside of town; why not test him with an eighteenth-century eyesore, a bowshot from your castle, and see what he can do to enliven it?

One would expect a children's mosque to be small. The Bala Hauz is instead a whole two-page spread of a porch facing out on a pool. (*Hauz* in Persian means "pool.") It is so tall that you need a fish-eye lens to bring it into focus (it quite conceals the mosque behind it). The Central Asians, it seems, have just rediscovered the virtues of paint. And up it goes, on the ceiling naturally, applied in carpetlike strips

Directly across from the citadel, or Ark, the emir's residence, is his private chapel, the Bala Hauz mosque. Twenty elongated wooden columns with *muqarnas* capitals form the loggia of this eighteenth-century structure. In front of it a small basin serves as a reflection pool.

between the beams, and in extraordinary, melting, fireworklike bursts over the three frontal arches. Supporting it all are two rows of columns shaped to look like royal palm trees. You could almost be in a Buddhist gompa, such is the feeling of freedom and, above all, delicacy that obtains amid this blaze of pattern.

The Summer Palace

Approaching the Museum of Regional Design, as the emir's Summer Palace is now billed, you may be excused for thinking that you have wandered into nothing more than a little avian zoo: there are peacocks, chukars, and a variety of Asian pheasants raucously calling out at you from inside their Soviet cages. This is not entirely illusion for, inside the palace, there they are again, this most royal of motifs, only now the peacock tails fan upward, broader and broader, the whole length of a tiled wall.

As your feet take you, clapping and cheering, from one triumph of kitsch to the next, you can't help but feel this is the magician's palace to end all magicians' palaces. An enormous white-on-white ganch-carved reception hall, a masterpiece of this uniquely Central Asian art, gives onto a room where the tricks now are of glass, extending from the eerie algae-green and crimson-stained tint of the windows right up to the mirrored ceiling. This room in turn leads into the Art Nouveau–influenced banquet hall, surely one of the wonders of the world, you exclaim, awed by the vastness of the yellow ceiling and the sumptuousness of the gilt-striped columns that carry the image of a tile frog with three eyes on each side of his head (green, blue, and brown and white), caught in a pink and blue arch. Another descending panel, yellow once again, ends in a glass-surrounded lilac-colored crown. This, in turn, gives onto a tall crimson-and-diamond glass chest of drawers. When accompanied by the emir's gold-plated service for fourteen, a peacock-clad footman in attendance behind each chair, and little pipes passing back and forth, all these twinkling, gleaming effects must have been quite delicious.

After dining the guests would have retired to the pavilion house across the garden—the emir had his harem in another building, as yet unrestored, overlooking a huge pool. Here, if you could distract yourself from the enticements of the stalactite-decorated ceiling and the niched walls with their peekaboo library, you would have retired to nap in one of several flower-tiled alcoves, under a crown of stars and starflowers winking down encouragingly from a milk-white vaulted ceiling.

Muradov's decadent melding of Art Nouveau and traditional Central Asian design is not the kind of architecture that travels well. At a proper distance you can feel almost grateful for a revolution that came along just in time to prevent any further excesses. Yet, wandering from one wondrous room to the next, it is hard not be struck by an open-mouthed excitement as if you had suddenly been wafted into some toucan-and-quetzal-bright tropical forest. The cry "Splendor—flight—lives" that wall after wall proclaims, may only represent the last gasp of an oligarchy shorn of any other self-justification. All the same you can't help but applaud the raucous-voiced courage evinced in this extraordinary twentieth-century palace.

The Nadir Divan-bigi madrasah (1622) is named for its patron, who was a vizier. Although it was built according to the traditional four-*iwan* plan, its façade decoration is unique: the spandrels of the *pishtaq* are ornamented by two phoenix-like birds *(simurgh)*.

PAGE 121
Part of an urban ensemble around the large pool known as Liabi Hauz, the Nadir Divan-bigi khanaqah stands directly across from the madrasah. It was also commissioned by the vizier. Its principal entrance faces the Liabi Hauz, creating a dramatic reflection.

The Liabi Hauz

The old town grew up around the Ark or royal citadel and the Tower of Death in what is today the southwest of the modern city. By the seventeenth century the population had grown so that a new town center, the Liabi Hauz, was built outside the walls. In this instance the pool is a very big square framed by giant four-hundred-year-old mulberry trees. On one side a series of steps—the tiny lips of *liabi?*—rises to the water-reflected arch of the Nadir Divan-bigi khanaqah. Across from this Sufi center, but set about a hundred yards back from the pool, is a madrasah, its great portal faced with a tile relief depicting a pair of dragon peacocks flying toward each other as if to embrace. A small park with trees, benches, and a sherbet parlor leads from the madrasah to the poolside restaurants, their bed tables, steps, and overhanging balconies all painted the same creamy turquoise. The whole scene, complete with the smells of outdoor cooking, the three geese waddling at your feet, the men in their various mufti lounging about on the bed tables, and the ancient music wailing down through the trees—each sob like the curve of an arch—could not be more pure Arabian Nights.

Having found a seat, you line up in front of one of the three kitchens. The first provides a stew, the second a marinated grilled chicken, while the third, an open-air affair, offers spicy dumplings along with the national rice dish, pelao. The pelao is served from an enormous conical trough. Taking an aluminum cooking pot in hand—it is what your serving will be weighed in—the cook scrapes up some carrots from the bottom of the trough, then ladles in a chunk or two of lamb, followed by a substantial helping of rice. A dollop of pomegranate juice, a final sprinkling of scallions and possibly raisins, and it is put on the scale—in Central Asia it is always quantity you are paying for—then served with a thick slice of bread that will double as a pusher.

A pelao's quality depends on the lamb's fat in which it is cooked. The so-called tail that the fat comes from is actually the part of the back that projects over the legs and sways with every movement of the lamb's body. It is instructive to watch the women in the market going from one 150-pound animal to the next, their practiced fingers pinching a tail here, removing a bit from the rear there and sniffing it, tasting it. In the Central Asian diet, fat is to a Sart what olive oil is to a Greek, or butter to a Norman. Everything is cooked in it. My Russian interpreter disapproved of the practice. So much grease could not be very good for you. But in such a dry climate you may need a certain intake of fat just to keep from withering away.

The vaulted entrance to the money changers' bazaar, Bukhara. The entrances to the *taqs* are marked by high *pishtaqs*.

The people themselves don't understand sheep without these "tails." One turn of the century traveler tells of a Sart who, at the sight of some sheep hanging in a Paris butcher shop, exclaimed in a tone of horror, "Why, they're dogs!"

Depositing the pelao at your table, you join two more queues: one across the square for some better bread; another for a pot of tea. In the old days you might have had a considerable choice, and merchants prided themselves on being able to tell a tea by the touch. Nowadays the only variety is green, grown in the Caucasus. It is spooned out generously, three pinches to a standard six-cup pot. And there is no question of not staying, seated at your table, until you have drained all of it.

Drinking tea in such circumstances can't help but be a form of meditation. In the first place the tea comes so scalding there is no way for even the thirstiest to gulp it down. You have to proceed slowly, as if it were a hot towel, not a cup, that you are drawing to your face, letting each sip adjust you that much more fully to the light, the heat, and those in their caftans and turbans and vests around you.

By now the tea is drinking you more than you are drinking it. Water, always so precious—life itself, those around you might say— is coursing through your veins. You feel yourself spreading out to meet its flow, becoming one with your sleeves, with all of the life circulating around you. Here, among the trees and the heat and the piercing music, conversation may be too difficult to attempt, but that doesn't mean you can't admire the shirt of the man seated across from you, its yellow and white stripes gaudier than anything out of Bond Street, partly because the stripes themselves are so much broader, partly because, as on so many of the shirts, there is a band of yellow cutting back on the diagonal at just the point where it can emphasize that seat of well-being, the paunch.

The bed table you are sitting on is a real bed, if bigger than those we tend to sleep on—a bed for six. It has metal designs on three sides resembling those of a headboard. The table is high enough so that dangling feet don't touch the ground. You don't squat so much as sprawl, Roman fashion, leaning back on your elbows and letting a leg jut out.

Suspended on this kind of a flying carpet, you find that exchanges can begin to happen in a way they don't when you are seated face-to-face on chairs, legs solidly planted on the ground. Who you are, each of you, is less important than the visual space, the ongoing picture, you create between you. Here I am helped by my status as that odd bird, a private traveler. The foreigners who descend on Bukhara are by and large package-tour folk. No sooner has the bus delivered them

than here it is scooping them up again. Even when it is parked the motor is always running, as if about to take off again, and you can see on their faces the panic it inspires: not so much fear of being left behind—no one in the Soviet Union is ever left behind—but of holding up the others, of upsetting some finely tuned schedule. They are, they can only be, their cameras, and you see them, even behind their moving bus windows, desperately clicking away.

A traveler with a pen and a packet of 4″ × 6″ cards sticking out of his back jeans pocket represents quite a different kettle of fish. Seizing the opportunity you show them these tools of your trade, the equivalent of their awl, their silversmith's scalpel. In a moment, such is the spirit of the place, they are offering to buy your watch, your sneakers, your jeans. Surely in jest, to see how you will react—they can't expect you to strip on the spot—but secretly you feel flattered. Were this your last stop you might even oblige them—anything to lighten your luggage.

Constructed in 1417, the Ulugh Beg madrasah in Bukhara is much smaller than its counterpart in Samarkand. Its high *pishtaq* is flanked by two stories of *iwan* loggias. Though some of the Kufic inscriptions on the façade are still intact, most of the mosaic revetment has been lost.

Religion

At first you are so astounded by this still-standing religious theater that you don't notice how unpeopled the sets are. The same, of course, might have been said of Samarkand. But there you could proceed on the not-unwarranted assumption that the mosques, madrasahs, and mausoleums were religious in name only, forms that the Timurids had co-opted for their own dynastic ends.

In Bukhara, however, for over a thousand years life revolved around one and only one end—religious edification. Bukhara was called Bukhara-e-Sherif, a title that infuses a distinct holiness into the "noble" by which it is usually rendered. It was for this religious theater that students came, drawn from all over the Muslim world. Of the 250 religious academies that adorned the town, today there is only one, the Mir Arab, in use. That it is one of only two in the whole of the Soviet Union may elicit a certain pride. But it is clear that the heart of Bukhara, of all that it existed for, has been summarily torn out. And it explains more than anything the rage the townsmen harbor toward almost any Russian visitor.

In the Soviet Union people are nominally free to worship as they please. And you do see colorfully dressed Muslims about the streets, proudly sporting the turbans in which they will be buried. But in a state-controlled economy, theirs is not the road to advancement, which is one reason why those you see are nearly all well advanced in years.

It would be wrong, however, to suppose that the Muslim faith is

Interior of the tomb chamber in the Mir Arab madrasah in Bukhara. Constructed in 1535–36, this madrasah is one of the few remaining active religious institutions in Soviet Central Asia. Located directly across from the Kalyan mosque, it takes its name from the famous sheikh whose tomb is found inside. The square chamber is crowned by a high cupola with arched ribbings. The use of *muqarnas* in the fan-shaped ribbings is typical of sixteenth-century construction.

Detail of an *iwan* in the courtyard of the Mir Arab madrasah. The *iwan's* vaulting is decorated with fan-shaped motifs and *muqarnas* ornamentation. The spandrels are covered in floral-patterned tile. A band of Koranic inscription in *thulth* script runs along the lower tier of the vaulting.

dying out. A religion without a priestly hierarchy and that doesn't insist on your proclaiming your faith every time a cock crows is one well equipped for survival. In this connection Gippenreiter's story about what he had to go through to photograph a service in a working mosque is germane. In requesting permission he pointed out that the service would not be disturbed, since neither he nor his camera would be visible. Despite these assurances neither the mosque's imam nor the state religious officials felt able to make a decision. Finally he was referred to the head people in the Bukhara Party hierarchy. After a certain amount of discussion they agreed, on the condition that he photograph the service from behind. "But that's not very interesting," Vadim protested. "People don't want to see row after row of backs." The officials were adamant; if he wanted to photograph a service, that was the only way it would be permitted. With no choice he went and took his photographs. When the service was over he could not have been more astonished to see coming out of the mosque the very Party officials with whom he had been negotiating. Obviously they did not want to risk losing their jobs.

With the Muslim population of the Soviet Union increasing at a rate that will make it the majority ethnic group by the year 2000, the nationality issue may well be the crucial one of the next decade. In

The Mir Arab's tomb chamber contains a number of cenotaphs. The sheikh's own cenotaph is marked by an engraved star.

an effort to probe it I called on the imam of the shrine of Ismail al-Bokhari, some twenty-five kilometers outside Samarkand. The shrine was recently built with privately raised funds and, with its plane tree–shaded pools and light and airy handcrafted interiors, it could not have been more serene.

The imam, dressed in the bluest of suits, was diplomacy itself, answering every question with a quotation from the Koran in the original Arabic. This was, he informed me, his first assignment. And he proceeded to tell me about al-Bokhari, whose collection of *hadith*—episodes from the life of the prophet—is second only to the Koran in religious authority. Born outside Bukhara around A.D. 809 and brought up by an educated mother, al-Bokhari was a true child prodigy. By the age of seven he had already memorized the whole of the Koran.

He was still in his teens when, with an end to finding out what he could about Mohammed and the origins of Islam, he set off on the travels that were to occupy the next forty years of his life. During this time he compiled seventeen books, including the *Shariya,* an eight-volume commentary on the Koran. When he finally returned to his native village, his renown was such that he attracted a considerable following. This annoyed the emir, who must have felt that there was room in Bukhara for only one theater—his own court. But the emir's efforts to lure al-Bokhari there to instruct his son in the Koran drew a pointed refusal from the holy wanderer: "Learning doesn't come to you, you have to come to it." This left the emir with no choice but to exile the saint. He came to the village where the shrine now stands and shortly thereafter died.

As the imam talked, batting compliments about like a Persian, it became clear that I was never going to find out what he actually thought. All he would say in answer to my questions was that he believed Islam would prevail—and throughout the world. As to when this might be, who knows? If 2,500 years of history have taught anything, it is that you can never afford to hurry your step.

One can understand Soviet sensitivity to questions of religious faith, especially in a region where the Russian presence dates back hardly more than a hundred years. Yet, however much one may dislike the destruction that the head-on attack on religion has caused, one has to acknowledge the positive contributions that the Soviet system has made in such areas as health, education, and female equality (the removal of the veil, for instance). Compare these people to their co-religionists in Iran, Afghanistan, and Pakistan, and they appear clearly better off. And it may only be when you have enough in your belly that you can begin to think as a people. All the same it is a very thin glue that binds together such diverse ethnic groups. One wonders whether there would still be any such thing as a Soviet Union without the charismatic figure of Lenin and his dream of a "brotherhood of the races."

Given the problem of assimilating so many minorities, one can see why in the early days of the revolution the Bolsheviks should have chosen to proscribe religion for its divisiveness. And it must be said that their efforts to substitute their own religion of "history" have not been entirely unsuccessful. Wherever you travel you cannot help but encounter young people for whom the study of, say, English is but a step toward an advanced degree in this historical "science" of theirs. But Central Asia and not Arabia or North Africa is the historic, most culturally conservative center of the Muslim world. And Islam is not the sort of religion that can be wiped out in a mere seventy years.

An Uzbek mullah.

Five times a day the faithful face Mecca and pray, but on Fridays Islam recommends joining a congregation in prayer. Though most of the Soviet Central Asian mosques no longer function, the faithful still carry out their duties.

The faithful leaving a mosque. The old men of Central Asia still congregate for Friday prayers, but many of the youth have lost their ties to their Muslim heritage.

Instead it is to be feared that in driving it underground the Soviets may have created an Islamic nationalism such as we have seen everywhere from Indonesia to Morocco, but which has never previously surfaced in Central Asia.

The Bazaar

In some ways the bazaars of Central Asia have hardly changed for hundreds of years. The excitement, the varied smells, and the bright colors are still there.

It doesn't take too much longer to view the monuments than the package tours allow. What do you do with the rest of your time—visit the Desert National Park, advertised by a camel poster in your hotel lobby? Well, you are told, it's no longer in operation. What does that mean, a friend asked, outraged. Have they trucked it off to Siberia? (A desert that won't someday bloom, even one of the dimensions of the Kyzyl Kum, is inconceivable to the Soviet imagination.) Then what about the two great sixteenth-century religious complexes, the Char Bakr, and the Behauddin, five and eight kilometers away, respectively? Off-limits, they are Muslim holy places. (On your last day, in the spirit of *glasnost,* you do persuade an off-duty driver to take you there, to find, of course, that there is hardly a person about, only a lot of new, already bulging brick restoration.)

When all else fails there is one place that always succeeds—the bazaar. Stay there long enough and you may get an inkling of what the society is all about.

The bazaar is worth visiting any day. But on a Sunday, when a quarter of a million people flood in from all over the region, there is nothing quite like it. Everywhere you look for much of a mile, spread out on bits of cloth, on fold-up aluminum cots, on the backs of carpet-draped trucks, a whole commercial labyrinth is on display—food, clothing, household goods of every description. In the noonday glare, and in the virtual absence of anything resembling an awning, it makes quite a spectacle.

At first the pressure of the milling crowds, of the lady vendors at your feet, of the goods hanging at every conceivable eye level, makes it hard to do anything but let yourself be shunted along, down one narrow aisle and up the next. But if there is no possibility for the moment of shopping you can gawk at the fronts and backs, at the beards, wispy mustaches, caps, and shawls of all those around you. And at the vendors who, here at least, do not have to conform to Soviet canons of dress. Everyone is in their most outrageous five-piece outfit, pattern zinging against pattern—why match when you can elate? And there is no thought of doffing a caftan, say, or a vest, just because the sun happens to be a little higher than when you set out.

Numerous teahouses (*chaikhaneh*) offer respite from the bustle of the bazaar. This man is enjoying a bowl of Central Asian green tea.

For those who cannot somehow tough it out there is always the teahouse. There on your bed table, among the odors of grilling carp and chickens you squat, eating with your fingers and hurling the dismemberments on the ground.

Pulled along by this gingerly shuffling current—you might as well be stepping over bodies at a beach—you start noticing the intricate

134

assembling that goes into any one outfit. The old, beautiful-eyed lady vendors seated so patiently on the ground are like old women the world over—paisley-shawled flowers. The younger ones favor something more boldly dissonant. This national sunburst, as I think of it, comes in any one of a number of background colors—black, green, etc. But what I have taken to be bands of vertical stripes is, I now see,

Men gather in teahouses to relax on bed tables *(takht)*, drink tea in a leisurely fashion, and discuss the great issues of the world.

135

Women's tunics, worn over colorfully printed *sharovary*, used to be fashioned from striped silks *(abri)* patterned with iridescent cloudlike shapes.

PAGE 137
The Central Asian sun is so strong that some form of head covering is essential.

PAGE 138
Older men still dress in traditional clothes: a cotton-padded overcoat, a caftan tied with a colorful sash, a tunic-like shirt, baggy pants, and a turban *(chalma)*.

Most men, young and old, wear embroidered skullcaps *(tiubeteika)*, which are much cooler than turbans. The women's skullcaps are more decorative and colorful than the men's.

a pattern of flowing pendants in which a band, say, of zebralike black and yellow drops onto a band of red, then black and yellow again, then white, the lightning flashes continuing down to the knees.

This highly vibrant clash of colors pales, however, before the extraordinary resonance of the bloomers. Visible only from the knee down (with, perhaps, exquisitely embroidered cuffs calling attention to the ends), the bloomers are nonetheless the centerpiece of every lady's costume, her fashion statement at its most chic. Add a vest or a long coat with silver-filigreed sleeves and a row or two of dangling, jingling breast ornaments, and she is more or less complete.

For men, especially those with the traditionally shaved skull, fash-

Even though a century has passed since Central Asia came under Russian rule, many people still wear traditional clothes. Women often cover their skullcap with a scarf.

ion turns on the quest for the perfect box cap. One does, of course, see their point; you are not shelling out for the eighteen meters of silk a turban requires. And in the summer the caps must be cooler than those great fur towers in which the Turkmen parade about. But they do seem to get worn out fast. Everywhere you look you see groups of men, or a man and his wife, turning them over, examining the inner stitching. Judging by the care of the scrutiny you understand that nothing less than a man's dignity is at stake.

Over their kohl-outlined eyes and long braids, or strands of braids, women may also wear a cap. Theirs come in a wider range of colors than the ubiquitous black and white of the men's. Covered in turn

A crowd gathers to inspect a vendor's wares.

Metalwork has long been a prized art in the Islamic world. The decoration on these contemporary copper and brass salvers is of extraordinary intricacy and richness.

with a shawl, the cap is what gives women that characteristic peaked look.

To the extent that your feet have a choice, you go on, drawn to wherever there is a crowd. What has fallen off the back of the Soviet truck? You espy a huddle of women and, taking a peep, you see— why, of course, children's plastic shoes. And here, to a roll of drums, in the middle of a ring, is a strongman lying on his back, asking to be crushed—don't you want to? And some ten, twenty of us good-naturedly stand on a board straddling his chest for what seems almost two minutes before the drums roll again and we hop off to go our separate ways.

In the old days I might have been tempted to buy the paper, made out of rags and parchmentlike in appearance, or the silver decorated with glass superimposed on strips of colored paper that make it seem to sparkle; or the height of traditional elegance, the gold-embroidered dresses that you still encounter on a weekend evening along the walkway to the Liabi Hauz pool. But my range is limited as I have only one medium-size suitcase and must still travel to Khiva. Every now and then from a tiny booth a recorded song wafts out irresistibly, and before anyone else can put his fingers on it I am there with pen and a blank piece of paper. That way there is no misunderstanding about the price. Then there is a knife, old Bukhara silver, clearly no bargain at $30, but with my pockets stuffed with unspendable rubles, it is probably worth that bit of a gulp. Aside from the silken shawls—often very old, and always luxuriously fringed—what attracts me are the turn-of-the-century neckties. They come already knotted, with an elastic band to fit around the neck, so that no more silk than necessary is wasted on them. But the color on the side that shows can be, like that of the one I purchased, a perfect peacock blue on to which a minor treasury of sequins has been sewn. If this is the one bit of fantasy a man is permitted it's hard to imagine anything that says it more persuasively.

Shopping here differs in that more than anything you are entering into a relationship. You are not just buying something, you are buying something from her, something that has been part of her. These squatting pawnshops, toughing it out in the parking-lot glare, a teapot near them as sole sustenance, can be of considerable age. As I pass one nonagenarian she thrusts up a boy's embroidered blue and gold jacket with a certainty that could not say more plainly, "Isn't this exactly what you have your heart set on?" I find it impossible not to agree and, squatting down beside her, hold out my pad. It turns out that she comes from a time before they learned to write, and after a certain amount of mutual bafflement, a young girl from a neighboring stand

Nuts and dried fruit have been valuable commodities for centuries. To be sure of getting the best quality, the buyer must taste the goods himself as the merchant looks on.

PAGE 145
Unlike the markets in Moscow and Leningrad, Central Asian markets offer an abundance of produce year round. These women are selling carrots, scallions, and other vegetables.

comes to our rescue. As is only fitting for such a treasure, certain numbers get written down, hers, mine, ping-pong. I pay and, because she can't make the change, the girl very kindly does it for us. When I turn around again after thanking her, the lady, money tucked into her bodice, has vanished. Obviously she has had her eye, these many Sundays, firmly fixed on a purchase of her own and now that she has the wherewithal has gone off to collect it.

By now the early afternoon sun is so blistering that most of the vendors are packing up. For those loath to join the scramble for taxis there is the shade of the covered fruit and vegetable market. Over the gateway, high in a tree, invisible birds chirp away in covered cages. Inside the fruit lies so copiously piled up that it is possible to make a small lunch by going from one mound to the next, plucking a handful of raisins here, some dried mulberries there. Such sampling is en-

An herb vendor.

Women selling flat cakes.

PAGES 148–49
Over 100 types of melon *(qawun)* are found in Central Asia. The hot, dry climate produces fruit of exceptional sweetness.

Women kneading dough to make flat cakes. The loaves are baked in special ovens called *tanurs*.

couraged if only because of the variety on offer—dried apricots of every conceivable shade of gold, raisins that may well be the tastiest on the planet. In the dry climate fruit keeps well and pomegranates can still be bought, along with watermelons arranged in hut-high mounds. Among the more unusual items are dried apricot pits and melon seeds that, ground into a nougatlike paste, will go into a flat cake.

At this time of year vegetables either are from last fall's crop or have been grown in a hothouse—a booming industry on every collective farm—but I am struck by the red scallions and the yellow carrots, a local delicacy (all the more surprising if you haven't reckoned on the several cloves of garlic with which they are invariably accompanied).

The Hamman

After the heat of the bazaar one would think a visit to a public bathhouse might be in order. Armed with the magic word *hammam* and a towel you can point at, you set off through the labyrinth. And eventually, after half an hour of "Where?" you find it, a multidomed building hardly distinguishable from any other, with separate entrances for men and women.

At this hour of the afternoon the locker room is relatively uncrowded, and there is an attendant about to make sure that you take your towel with you into the bath. You use it as you would a washcloth, lathering yourself with the soap from the basin that you carry about with you. For water there are a pair of showers and various spigots that, given the right sequence of taps, will sputter forth. All around you steam is rising, so much so that the steps leading to a second domed sauna are quite invisible. But you see a wraith coming down them, and up you go for some even hotter steam. When you return a few minutes later, blinking unaccustomed eyes at the light, you notice a score of figures, most of them exceedingly corpulent, spread out on one or another tile bench. They are waiting to be kneaded. Someone pummels away at your arms, back, and shoulders, then in the Soviet manner you return the favor. After it is over no one would dream of speeding things up with a towel. You just sit until dry enough to venture out in the street. But you do notice how welcome all this air is in which you stroll.

Tass

Near the end of my stay in Bukhara a man from Tass comes to interview me for the local paper. The interview passes through the usual narrow defiles: Lenin—his 118th birthday is two days away; the approaching Reagan-Gorbachev summit meeting; Afghanistan, which, he announces, has just been solved in Geneva. "Solved," I ask, raising my eyebrows, "only as far as America and the Soviet Union are concerned—what about the Afghans?" Finally the parting question: What, by way of friendship, do you wish for the people of Central Asia? One word stands out for me. I say it: "Autonomy." There is a moment of silence. Apparently autonomy is not a word that translates well. "What sort of autonomy?" the translator asks, trying to save something. But I can't think of an adjective, and on this brilliant note our interview ends.

Domed roofs of a bathhouse. Bathhouses are a staple of Islamic cities, a tradition that probably derives from ancient Greece. The baths used to be composed of a number of chambers. According to a nineteenth-century traveler, in the first chamber the visitor took off his upper clothing. In the second, where the temperature was warmer, the rest of his clothing was removed, and he was wrapped in a *lung*, or bathing girdle. In the third and hottest room, the bather sat until he had worked up a good sweat, and in the fourth chamber he was massaged, rubbed with coarse haircloth, and rinsed with cold water. He then returned to the second chamber to rest and drink tea.

The camel is food, drink, transport, clothing, and shelter to the nomads of the desert.

The salt marshes of the Badkhyz Reserve in Turkmenia at sunset.

The desolate, wind-eroded saline hollows of
the Kara Kum desert create dramatic
landscapes.

The first flowering of spring in the desert.

The windswept dunes of the Repetek Preserve form striking compositions.

✳ KHIVA ✳

The way to arrive in Khiva is, of course, by caravan. After twenty days spent crossing the infamous Kara Kum desert, the City of Nightingales must have looked like the very image of paradise. Of the belt of green surrounding the city, the early nineteenth-century traveler Muraviev remarked that he had never seen countryside so intensively cultivated, even in Germany. But the beauty of the "numberless" gardens hardly compared with the architectural spectacle provided by the towering monuments of the walled inner city, the Ichan Qala or Royal Court. Based as the prosperity was, however, on the violence of the slave trade—and anyone passing was fair game—approaching the great gates of the Ichan Qala could not have helped but send a definite chill down any visitor's spine.

If you can't arrive by caravan, the next best thing might be by train from Bukhara. The Kyzyl Kum is not quite the Kara Kum, but two nights and a day of it might acquaint you with a variety of Turkmen faces, hats, blankets, and jewelry. And the great spaces themselves, those gaunt saksaul elms and sensuous dunes of Gippenreiter's photographs, might give you a chance to reflect on how even the 1874 conqueror of Khiva, General Kaufmann, and his army would have perished but for a scout's chance finding of a well fifty miles away. So when the Intourist lady at my Moscow hotel told me that that was how I'd be traveling I was elated. In other countries trains have at best a certain curiosity value. In the Soviet Union they offer a true celebration of life, akin, from all reports, to following the Tour de France in Europe.

When, however, my schedule finally came through I learned that I would be traveling by air. Various pretexts were given to me: the train was not a very good one, there were only four sleeping compartments, not to mention the heat through which I would even in early spring be passing. Mother Intourist may have been right in wanting to spare my sensibilities. But I suspect the real reason behind this and other similar refusals may have been financial: Intourist would not be earning any hard currency while I was off touring the desert courtesy of the railways.

So here I was, plopped down out of the desert sky on Urgench, some forty minutes by car from Khiva, and where you are required to stay if you are a foreigner. (There is a hotel made out of a converted religious academy in Khiva proper, but it's for Russians only.) "What, no group?" the airport taxi driver asked, eyeing this pariah with a look of the most withering scorn. And for a moment as we drove through modern Urgench, a city built on the soulless monster-block Stalinist grid, it struck me that I might have some trouble making the daily commute to Khiva.

An Uzbek.

PAGE 156
Panorama of the Ichan Qala (Inner City) of Khiva from the Kalta Minar, known as the Short or Green Tower. Khiva's enchanting skyline of towering minarets and colorful domes rivals that of Samarkand and Bukhara. Founded by Ilbars the Shaybanid in 1512, it became the capital of the Turkish khanate in the seventeenth century.

157

Cotton has become the symbol of Uzbekistan. Formerly this white gold was used to make costly paper for the Islamic world.

Fortunately there were public conveyances. Seventy-five people with all their effects crammed into a forty-five-seat bus might sound all too cozy, but it was instructive to see, as we passed a cemetery, every person drop everything he or she was carrying to run both hands over the face in the traditional gesture. Here, at least, Big Brother wasn't watching.

The orchards and gardens with their nightingales may have vanished for the nonce—cotton is even more dominant than in Bukhara—but the three-mile walk from the bus terminal by the outer city gate to the Ichan Qala gave me the chance to study the faces, which are of a more pronounced Asiatic cast—some you could easily mistake for Korean—than I had so far come upon. In late April, under an overcast sky—it's the so-called rainy season, though hardly a drop falls—the walk could not have been more pleasant, revealing an intensity of green, of tree-lined canals and streets such as I have never encountered in a Central Asian city. But I had only to look at the houses' north-facing courtyards with their tall, slanted, three-quarter-covered roofs to sense the ferocity that has brought this unique ventilating system into being.

It is the massively walled Ichan Qala, however, that captures the eye, both by its scale and by a coherence of effect that does not have its like in the Moslem world. For once you do not feel you are piecing together the scraps of a hopelessly obliterated puzzle. And the presence within a twenty-two-hectare enclosure of so much monumental building, nearly all of one period (1780–1850), cannot be more impressive: the six towers lined up on a single axis; the entrance portals projecting forth from their raised platforms, their huge façades dropping abruptly onto sunken alleys; streets twisting hither and thither to catch every particle of wind or shadow. Every few steps throws up a new perspective: domes, tree-shaded squares, views plunging out over the walls onto the surrounding green. The theatricality that every Central Asian city aims at is realized here to an unparalleled degree.

Yet the mood that emanates from the buildings is one of a wary severity, a reminder of the city's garrison origins and above all of the slave trade to which it owed its nineteenth-century prosperity.

Khiva came into being in the tenth century as a desert fortress protecting the caravan trail that linked the once huge city of Merv (a million-and-a-half population) with the Aral Sea. And it was as a second fortress within Khiva proper that the Ichan Qala grew, affording a place of refuge for the oasis dwellers during periods of internecine warfare and, for the rulers themselves, a stronghold against any popular insurrection.

Burial places in the walls
of the Ichan Qala.

View of Khiva from the Kalta Minar, looking
toward one of the largest ensembles in the
Ichan Qala.

View of the city from the Kalta Minar, looking toward the Islam Khwaja madrasah.

The drum-shaped Kalta Minar in the foreground and the Islam Khwaja Minar in the distance. The numerous courtyards of the Ichan Qala create open spaces in an otherwise tight urban fabric.

One of Khiva's narrow streets. The entrance to the caravanserai of Alla-Quli Khan (1832–33) is on the right, the Tash Hauli palace on the left.

A typical street in Khiva.

The vaulted rooftops of Khiva. In the distance is the dome of the Islam Khwaja madrasah.

At the time, however, the capital of the Khwarezm region was Urgench, a considerably different Urgench than I landed in and situated some two hundred kilometers away. Ibn Batuta remembered it as the "greatest, most beautiful, and most important city of the Turks." What impressed him most when he visited it in 1331 was the seething mass of the throngs, "whose movements lend it the semblance of a billowy sea." As a center of piety and religious learning the city ranked second only to Bukhara. Among its more renowned luminaries was the mathematician al-Khwarezmi—he who gave us our square roots and quadratic equations. The surrounding oasis was famed for the quality of its

A twelfth-century mausoleum in Kunya Urgench (Old Urgench).

165

Detail of the Tekesh mausoleum in Kunya Urgench, famed for its ornate brickwork and glazed terra-cotta inscriptions.

The mausoleum of the Khwarezmian King Tekesh (twelfth century) in Kunya Urgench. Its composition and highly ornate decoration are characteristic of Khwarez-mian architecture before the Mongol invasion. The coni-cal-shaped outer dome surmounts an inner cupola. Other examples of Khwarezm's artistic tradition are the tall minaret, which has lost its upper part, and the Tyerbeg-Khanum mausoleum in the distance. Perhaps it was these buildings that induced Timur to import Khwarez-mian craftsmen to his birthplace.

The bazaar in Khiva is not very far from the caravanserai of Alla-Quli Khan.

melons. Wrapped in individual leather casings, they were sent out by camel caravan to adorn the tables of princes.

Such prosperity attracted the inevitable looters. Genghis Khan razed Urgench in 1221 after the heroic twelve-day resistance of 12,000 men against a horde of 600,000. And Timur razed it no less than five times, surely a Central Asian record. By the last time he was so exasperated that he had the remaining inhabitants carted away as slaves and ordered barley to be sown through the city's streets.

However, it was not these razings but the city's vulnerability to the Amu Darya that was to spell its eventual doom. The filth and stench caused by the river's flooding is attested to by a score of travelers. Worse than the inundations was the Amu Darya's tendency to shift its banks—as much as sixty kilometers—leaving the inhabitants little choice but to follow after it. After a number of such shiftings Urgench was finally abandoned in the seventeenth century.

The Slave Trade

By then Khiva was beginning to develop what became the biggest slave market in Central Asia, a function of the symbiotic relationship that normally holds in an oasis between the inhabitants and the surrounding nomads. Khwarezm nomads were Turkmen who had migrated east out of Anatolia at the end of the ninth century. Along with falcons, furs, fast horses, and carpets as beautiful as any in the world, it was perhaps only natural that a continuing trade should develop in human bodies. The business of households lay in extracting whimpers, groans, and anything that, put into an envelope and entrusted to a caravan, might lead to a quicker ransom. Vambéry, who lived in constant fear of having his disguise penetrated and sharing this fate, gives a harrowing account of the considerable variety of tortures inflicted as a matter of business. But families aren't all equally sensitive to a kinsman's confessions of pain, let alone the odd ear or finger stub, and the Khiva slave market developed to dispose of those who couldn't be ransomed.

The slave trade was not without the occasional hiccup. In 1715, as a consequence of having defeated a Persian army, the khan finds himself in possession of a number of prisoners. Since Persians are the acknowledged master craftsmen of Central Asia, he decides to put this talent to work by having them build him an academy. It would give him a place to house the Russian mission being sent by Peter the Great, with whom he has been secretly negotiating. The Persians agree on the condition that they be allowed to return to their homes when the

The *chaikhaneh* provides respite from the blistering sun.

building is finished. But the khan is so taken by the elegance of their work that he begins to have second thoughts about losing such a valuable work force. Perhaps they might build him something else? As can be imagined, this reneging doesn't go over well with the Persians. One day, as he is hemming and hawing as usual, one of them picks up a brick, others follow suit, and before anyone can intervene the khan has been stoned to death.

The Russian emissaries, meanwhile, have been advancing across the saltscapes. When they arrive they find a new khan installed. He cannot make head or tail of the negotiations they keep referring to and in a fit of exasperation has them all slain. Their heads are then sent back to the czar on an enormous silver platter.

Here matters rest until 1740, when the last great Persian conqueror of modern times, Nadir Shah, arrives at the head of a considerable

169

Women selling brooms at the Khiva bazaar.

A cooling breeze and a bit of shade must be welcome to these women returning from the bazaar.

army. A Turkman himself—he is reputed to have murdered five brothers on his way to the Peacock Throne—he is determined to put an end to the slave business, which exists mainly at his subjects' expense. The devastation he inflicts is so effective that even twenty years later there are only forty families living in Khiva, and wild animals may be seen prowling the ruins.

In Central Asia cities rise from their ashes faster and better than in most other places. Khiva's irrigation system is restored, new bazaars are built, and trade is opened with Bukhara, Persia, and Russia. The basis of the new prosperity is the slave trade. During the first half of the nineteenth century a million people are snatched from Persia alone. Fueled by this new labor pool—there are fifty to sixty thousand slaves in Khiva—the Ichan Qala as we know it comes into being. Just as a robber baron might salve his conscience by endowing a university chair or a civic auditorium, so the khan's merchants and generals vie to erect madrasahs; in the Ichan Qala alone there are twenty-two of these academies, or one per hectare.

Workmanship

In Bukhara and Samarkand there may be some local techniques at work, notably in ganch carving, but the finished product is recognizably neo-Persian. In Khiva one can't help but be struck by a change of idiom. One might still be in Greater Persia as far as the basic architectural forms are concerned. But there is no sense of craftsmen looking over their shoulders at what is being done elsewhere, and the work itself is considerably finer.

One sign of this new confidence can be seen in the expanded role given to tile paneling. By comparison with contemporary Bukhara, the use of color may seem rather curtailed: no reds, oranges, greens, yellows, or blacks. Even turquoise, the dominant color of Samarkand and Bukhara, appears here only as a highlight, the odd teardrop on the ribbing of an arch. In effect, the Khivans are no longer thinking color,

Interior of the Juma mosque (1788–89). The foundation of Khiva's Friday mosque dates back to the tenth century. This hypostyle (multi-pillared) mosque was built to accommodate the entire male population of Khiva. Its 212 wooden columns are placed at equal distances and three openings in the ceiling allow light into the mosque. A number of the wooden columns date back to the tenth–sixteenth centuries. Some have inscriptions and others are decorated with exquisite carvings.

but design. Everything is now done in tile panels, following a medallion design that plays off center and border against each other. And the individual panels are remarkably varied; in the whole of the Ichan Qala it is rare to find two alike.

Where this medallion technique derives from is anybody's guess. And the panel techniques that I am struck by could have come from any number of sources, even a design manual brought back from a pilgrimage. There also may be a crossover from the art of wood carving, which reaches a subtlety here that is unsurpassed in Central Asia. In this respect the Juma Mosque's forest of columns, many of them saved from the ruins of Urgench, must have provided a considerable repertoire of forms from which to draw.

If we can't pin down the sources, much of the credit for the innovation, I think, can be assigned to one man, Abdullah Djinn. (Perhaps the "djinn" sobriquet suggests that his designs had a bit of the devil in them.) Whenever a panel strikes you as really marvelous you can be sure that he or his brother had a hand in it.

Fragment of a door in the Kurinish Khaneh (throne or reception room) of the Kunya Ark, at one time the emir's palace. The model for the Kurinish Khaneh was the typical Khwarezmian dwelling with a double-pillared *iwan*. The elaborate fretwork on this door demonstrates the high art of woodcarving in Khwarezm.

The Pahlavan Mahmoud Mausoleum

Abdullah's masterpiece is the Pahlavan Mahmoud mausoleum (1810–25). It was built to commemorate a twelfth-century poet and undefeated wrestler of the same Koungrat family as the ruling khan. Mahmoud was deeply influenced by Omar Khayyám. The rubâ'i inscribed over his tomb would strike a chord in anyone who has tried to teach in a public school: "It is far easier to spend a hundred years in jail, to climb a hundred mountains, than to try to persuade a stupid person of the truth."

In the earlier tile work of Samarkand and Bukhara, the dominant image is that of the afterlife rendered as a spring meadow. And like a meadow we want it to go on and on, from wall to wall and arch to arch. As it does so, individuality inevitably gives way to the play of color, the ever-changing kaleidoscope of blues, greens, oranges, reds. Yet this outburst of color—dawn, sunlight, floral waves dancing—can't help but make us aware of the greater rhythm governing it, of our being in the presence of a single, miraculously sustained breath. The tile depicts, in other words, not a real world, but the garden of faith, the paradise awaiting the true believer.

The gardens, the night skies that Abdullah conjures up are no

173

Exterior of the ensemble of Pahlavan Mahmoud, the revered twelfth-century wrestler, furrier, and poet who has become known as Khiva's protector. Over the centuries other buildings were constructed around his fourteenth-century tomb. In 1810 Mohammed Rahim Khan ordered the construction of a new mausoleum.

The courtyard of the Pahlavan Mahmoud ensemble as seen from the gatehouse, the *darwazeh khaneh*, built by Shah-Niyaz Khan in 1701, according to inscriptions on the door. To the left is a hall that served as a burial vault for the khans of Khiva.

175

PAGE 176
Dome of the *ziaratkhaneh* (visitation chamber) in the Pahlavan Mahmoud. The exquisite tile decoration in the ensemble is the work of the craftsmen Sufi Mohammed—the son of Usta Abdul Jabbar—and Abdullah Djinn.

The *dakhma,* or gravestone, of Isfandiyar Khan. The two-story Isfandiyar Khan mausoleum was constructed in 1913 in the courtyard of the Pahlavan Mahmoud. Tile decoration of variegated vegetal and geometric designs covers the multitiered cenotaph and interior walls of the burial chamber.

more real than those of traditional neo-Persian art, but the design is no longer static. Standing within it you feel as if you have been caught up in an immense hammered tray. Colors are all around you, echoing, pounding, but it's not color that you are taking in so much as design—a restless swirling that seems to be pulling you every which way at once. The effect of the gardens, the starflowers, is no longer one of profusion, but speed. And nothing in the surrounding architecture is allowed to get in the way of this dizzying, vertiginous movement. Thus the indented arches are there for form's sake only, tiny by comparison with what we usually see, and placed low in the corners where the eye can vault over them to the great gonglike medallions of the six-triangled dome. It's not so much a hypnotic effect that Abdullah is after as one of amazement, and maybe of a certain mystical darkness, the awe a star-studded sky evokes.

The Islam Khwaja madrasah. Detail of the
pishtaq, constructed by Islam Khwaja, the
vizier of Isfandiyar Khan, in 1908–10. The
high *pishtaq* has masterful tile decoration.

The Tash Hauli

Abdullah also worked on the Ichan Qala's other great building, the 163-room Tash Hauli or Stone Palace. Built between 1830 and 1838, it is a fort within the fort of the Ichan Qala and features elements of rural architecture (turrets, crenellated walls, little strongholds) within a series of separately enclosed compounds.

In commissioning his architect, Nour, all the khan wanted was a palace grander and more beautiful than any other in Central Asia. And he must have imagined that, with so many slaves about, all the architect had to do was crack the whip for it to be finished in a maximum of two years. As the months dragged on, with no sign of its ever being ready, the khan became understandably impatient. Finally he was left with no choice but to insist that if the palace wasn't finished on time Nour would pay with his head. When Nour bravely protested that it

Detail of an *iwan* in the harem of the Tash Hauli. One of the emir's palaces in the Ichan Qala, the Tash Hauli included both ceremonial reception halls *(deshan-hauli)* and private quarters *(ichan-hauli)*. Constructed in numerous phases between the years 1830 and 1838, the Tash Hauli replaced the Kunya Ark as the emir's residence. The word *hauli* means country seat. Single-pillared *iwans* such as this one are characteristic of Khwarezmian architecture. The blue-and-white tilework in vegetal and geometric motifs is particularly Khivan.

Detail of the base of a column in the Tash Hauli.

The *iwans* in the Tash Hauli palace are supported by tall, slender wooden columns, with elaborately decorated bases. The columns' fretwork and carved designs repeat patterns found on the tile revetment.

One of the first buildings to be erected in the Tash Hauli was the harem, which is separated from the public quarters by a long corridor. The single-pillared *iwans* face the open courtyard of the harem and have intricate colorful tile decoration, the work of master craftsman Abdullah Djinn.

181

The elaborately carved wooden columns and colorful tile decoration of the Tash Hauli were supplemented by the artistry of Khwarezmian stonemasons, as these details of the façade (top) and of the base of a column (bottom) attest. In the base of the column the mason has repeated in marble the *muqarnas* of an arch.

couldn't be done, not even with the whole city working day and night, the khan, true to his word, had him executed. Even so, it took another ten years to complete the palace.

Most of the Tash Hauli is still being restored, work that is expected to continue for several more years, and it was only possible to see the harem. But then a compound of such privacy, one to which only the khan and his eunuchs would have had access, can give an unparalleled view of a civilization at its most intimate.

The courtyard into which you enter is the size of a small soccer field, large enough to accommodate the felt tents in which the inhabitants passed the winter. On the left are five open-sided rooms, the first for the khan, the others for his four wives. All are tiled in blue, their painted ceilings supported by individually carved, marble-based wooden columns. Each room leads off into a boudoir behind it. All around the courtyard are horizontal panels of blue and white tile strewn about like carpets—a limited use of color that must have been relieved by that of the silken costumes, the sounds of instruments being plucked, and the inevitable dancing.

The Kalta Minar

No sooner is the Tash Hauli complete than the khan decides to erect a tower that in size and in the splendor of its façade will surpass anything in Central Asia. This tower is the Kalta Minar, variously known as the Short or Green Tower. Judging by the 1908 Islam-Khwaja watchtower that replaced it, it must have served a military function. One can imagine how useful such a tower would have been in receiving messages from the garrison outposts, in spotting caravans and raiding parties of Turkmen, and, most important, in keeping tabs on the local citizenry.

Word of such a structure was bound to travel fast, and one can see the emir of Bukhara wanting a spy in the sky of those same dimensions, those same radiantly changing greens and blues. Legend has it that he invited the tower's master builder to come to Bukhara and build him one. Unfortunately, news of the offer soon reached the ears of the khan. He was furious. You don't go to the trouble of erecting the world's tallest tower only to have it pirated by your principal competitor. The only fitting punishment was to have his betrayer executed by being thrown from the top of the Kalta Minar. Alas, the master builder survived the fall—in what state we are not told. Normally such a survival would be considered an act of God and the criminal allowed

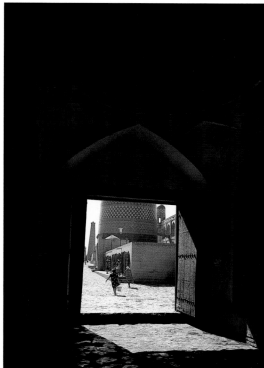

View of the Kalta Minar from the Ata Darwazeh, one of Khiva's gates.

Minaret and madrasah of Islam Khwaja. Forty-two student cells surround the courtyard of the madrasah. Only the main façade is two-storied, the other three sides are single-storied. The minaret (1908–10) is ringed by decorative bands of tile revetment.

View of the Kalta Minar and the Mohammed Amin Khan madrasah (1851–52). Intended to be the tallest minaret in Central Asia, the Kalta Minar would have reached 265 feet, had construction not been interrupted by the khan's death in 1855. Only 98 feet high, the minaret was dubbed *Kalta*, for its short size. The adjacent madrasah was one of the largest theological schools built in this period.

to go free. But the khan was adamant, and the master builder was hauled to the top of the tower and thrown off a second time. This was too much for the tower's workmen. They walked off the job and nobody could ever be found to replace them. What visual heights the tower might have reached is tantalizing to imagine (the blues and greens of the tile are just beginning to intensify). Even so it remains in its drum-like state the most arresting structure on the Khiva skyline.

The Kalta Minar marks one of the last achievements in the theatrical vein. By the time Vambéry passes through in 1863, the building has come to a virtual halt, and we find the khan preoccupied with writing more and more flowery letters to Queen Victoria, as if Her Majesty, or some military advisors sent out by her—the British are, after all, in Afghanistan—could save Khiva from the advancing Russians. But does the "Sun of the Sky of Exaltedness and Fortune, the Jewel of the Sea of Glory and Greatness . . . Chief among Sovereigns of the Messiah's Faith" deign to reply? No, the letter, in spite of Stoddart's accompanying dispatch to Lord Palmerston, never gets answered, much less, one suspects, read, and with it perishes Britain's final chance of stopping the Russian advance somewhere north of the Amu Darya.

Samarkand capitulates in the 1850s, Bukhara in 1868. Finally, in 1873, it is Khiva's turn. Sensing the end of an era, correspondents from all over Christendom descend on the city to cover the event. Some, like Englishman David Ker, fall victim to the terrain, but Ker nevertheless manages to publish *On the Road to Khiva,* complete with photographs and military map. The *New York Herald's* MacGahan, to his vast credit, does make it, and his sprightly account of his solo ride in *Campaigning on the Oxus and the Fall of Khiva* goes into three editions and remains a travel classic.

So the last bastion of Central Asia falls. Or the next to last since the Teke fortress of Geok Tepe is not taken until 1881.

Once a theater's lights have dimmed it may be quite a while before they can be turned up again. But within their limited mandate the Soviets have certainly tried. While one may not always care for their way of creating a "museum in the open," the sanitized cordon sealing off the great sets from so much of their former life, one can't help but be impressed by the scale of the public resources being committed and the thoroughness of the restoration. The cities are not yet the gardens that our imaginations need. But a number of historically important sets have been saved from oblivion. It even seems possible that this time the curtain will go up without recourse to the violence that originally generated it.

A twelfth-century mausoleum in Kunya Urgench
silhouetted against the setting sun.

BIBLIOGRAPHY

Beard, Michael. "European Travelers in the Trans-Caspian before 1917." *Cahiers du monde russe et soviétique* 13, no. 4 (1972), 590–596.

Bennigsen, Alexandre, and Wimbush, S. Enders. *Muslims of the Soviet Empire*. London, 1985.

Brodsky, Joseph. "Flight from Byzantium." In *Less Than One: Selected Essays*. New York, 1986.

Byron, Robert. *The Road to Oxiana*. London, 1981.

Clavijo, Gonzales de. *Embassy to Tamerlane*. Translated by Guy Le Strange. London, 1928.

De Gaury, Gerald, and Winstone, H.V.F. *The Road to Kabul*. London, 1981.

Gobineau, J. A. *Tales of Asia*. Translated by J. Lewis May. London, 1947.

Grabar, Oleg. *Islamic Architecture and Its Decoration*. London, 1967.

Ibn Batuta. *Travels in Asia and Africa, 1325–1354*. London, 1983.

Jenkinson, Anthony. *A Compendious . . . Declaration of the Journey of M.A.J. from . . . London into the land of Persia . . . anno 1561*. London, 1598–1600.

Ker, David. *On the Road to Khiva*. London, 1874.

Knobloch, Edgar. *Beyond the Oxus*. London, 1982.

Lamb, Harold. *Tamerlane, the Earth Shaker*. New York, 1928.

Maillart, Ella. *Turkestan Solo*. Translated by John Rodker. London, 1985.

MacGahan, J. A. *Campaigning on the Oxus and the Fall of Khiva*. New York, 1970.

Maclean, Fitzroy. *To the Back of Beyond: An Illustrated Companion to Central Asia and Mongolia*. London, 1934.

Meakin, Annette M. B. *In Russian Turkestan*. London, 1915.

Muraviev, M. N. *Visit to the Turcoman Inhabitants of the Eastern Shore Coast of the Caspian Sea*. London, 1871.

Olufsen, Axel Frits Olaf Henrik. *The Emir of Bokhara and his Country*. London, 1911.

Pahlen, Count K. K. *Mission to Turkestan, Being the Memoirs of Count K. K. Pahlen, 1908–09*. Translated by N. J. Couriss. London, 1964.

Pope, A. U. *A Survey of Persian Art*. London, 1939.

Pugachenkova, G. A. *A Museum in the Open*. Tashkent, 1981.

Schuyler, Eugene. *Turkistan: Notes of a Journey in Russian Turkistan, Khokand, Bukhara, and Kuldja*. New York, 1877.

Vambéry, Arminius. *Travels in Central Asia; Being the Account of a Journey from Teheran Across the Turkoman Desert on the Eastern Shore of the Caspian to Khiva, Bokhara, and Samarcand performed in the year 1863*. London, 1864.

Wolff, Joseph. *Narrative of a Mission to Bokhara in the Years 1843–1845 To Ascertain the Fate of Colonel Stoddart and Captain Conolly*. Edinburgh, 1852.

Z., Y. *From Moscow to Samarkand*. London, 1932.

INDEX

Note: Page numbers in *italics* refer to photographs.